MW01249127

PHRASEBOOK

— CZECH —

THE MOST IMPORTANT PHRASES

This phrasebook contains
the most important
phrases and questions
for basic communication
Everything you need
to survive overseas

By Andrey Taranov

T&P BOOKS

Phrasebook + 1500-word dictionary

English-Czech phrasebook & concise dictionary

By Andrey Taranov

The collection of "Everything Will Be Okay" travel phrasebooks published by T&P Books is designed for people traveling abroad for tourism and business. The phrasebooks contain what matters most - the essentials for basic communication. This is an indispensable set of phrases to "survive" while abroad.

Another section of the book also provides a small dictionary with more than 1,500 useful words arranged alphabetically. The dictionary includes a lot of gastronomic terms and will be helpful when ordering food at a restaurant or buying groceries at the store.

T&P Books Publishing
www.tpbooks.com

ISBN: 978-1-78492-441-6

This book is also available in E-book formats.
Please visit www.tpbooks.com or the major online bookstores.

FOREWORD

The collection of "Everything Will Be Okay" travel phrasebooks published by T&P Books is designed for people traveling abroad for tourism and business. The phrasebooks contain what matters most - the essentials for basic communication. This is an indispensable set of phrases to "survive" while abroad.

This phrasebook will help you in most cases where you need to ask something, get directions, find out how much something costs, etc. It can also resolve difficult communication situations where gestures just won't help.

This book contains a lot of phrases that have been grouped according to the most relevant topics. A separate section of the book also provides a small dictionary with more than 1,500 important and useful words.

Take "Everything Will Be Okay" phrasebook with you on the road and you'll have an irreplaceable traveling companion who will help you find your way out of any situation and teach you to not fear speaking with foreigners.

TABLE OF CONTENTS

Pronunciation   5
List of abbreviations   6
English-Czech phrasebook   7
Concise Dictionary   71

T&P Books Publishing

PRONUNCIATION

T&P phonetic alphabet	Czech example	English example
[a]	lavina [lavɪna]	shorter than in ask
[aː]	banán [banaːn]	calf, palm
[e]	beseda [bɛsɛda]	elm, medal
[ɛː]	chléb [xlɛːp]	longer than bed, fell
[ɪ]	Bible [bɪblɛ]	big, America
[iː]	chudý [xudiː]	feet, meter
[o]	epocha [ɛpoxa]	pod, John
[oː]	diagnóza [dɪagnoːza]	fall, bomb
[u]	dokument [dokumɛnt]	book
[uː]	chůva [xuːva]	pool, room
[b]	babička [babɪt͡ʃka]	baby, book
[t͡s]	celnice [t͡sɛlnɪt͡sɛ]	cats, tsetse fly
[t͡ʃ]	vlčák [vlt͡ʃaːk]	church, French
[x]	archeologie [arxɛologɪe]	as in Scots 'loch'
[d]	delfín [dɛlfiːn]	day, doctor
[dʲ]	Holanďan [holandʲan]	median, radio
[f]	atmosféra [atmosfɛːra]	face, food
[g]	galaxie [galaksɪe]	game, gold
[h]	knihovna [knɪhovna]	huge, hat
[j]	jídlo [jiːdlo]	yes, New York
[k]	zaplakat [zaplakat]	clock, kiss
[l]	chlapec [xlapɛt͡s]	lace, people
[m]	modelář [modɛlaːrʒ]	magic, milk
[n]	imunita [ɪmunɪta]	name, normal
[nʲ]	báseň [baːsɛnʲ]	canyon, new
[ŋk]	vstupenka [vstupɛŋka]	bank, trunk
[p]	poločas [polot͡ʃas]	pencil, private
[r]	senátor [sɛnaːtor]	rice, radio
[rʒ], [rʃ]	bouřka [bourʃka]	urgent, flash
[s]	svoboda [svoboda]	city, boss
[ʃ]	šiška [ʃɪʃka]	machine, shark
[t]	turista [turɪsta]	tourist, trip
[tʲ]	poušť [pouʃtʲ]	tune, student
[v]	veverka [vɛvɛrka]	very, river
[z]	zapomínat [zapomiːnat]	zebra, please
[ʒ]	ložisko [loʒɪsko]	forge, pleasure

LIST OF ABBREVIATIONS

English abbreviations

ab.	-	about
adj	-	adjective
adv	-	adverb
anim.	-	animate
as adj	-	attributive noun used as adjective
e.g.	-	for example
etc.	-	et cetera
fam.	-	familiar
fem.	-	feminine
form.	-	formal
inanim.	-	inanimate
masc.	-	masculine
math	-	mathematics
mil.	-	military
n	-	noun
pl	-	plural
pron.	-	pronoun
sb	-	somebody
sing.	-	singular
sth	-	something
v aux	-	auxiliary verb
vi	-	intransitive verb
vi, vt	-	intransitive, transitive verb
vt	-	transitive verb

Czech abbreviations

ž	-	feminine noun
ž mn	-	feminine plural
m	-	masculine noun
m mn	-	masculine plural
m, ž	-	masculine, feminine
mn	-	plural
s	-	neuter
s mn	-	neuter plural

CZECH
PHRASEBOOK

This section contains
important phrases that may
come in handy in various
real-life situations.
The phrasebook will help
you ask for directions, clarify
a price, buy tickets, and
order food at a restaurant

T&P Books Publishing

PHRASEBOOK
CONTENTS

The bare minimum 10
Questions 13
Needs 14
Asking for directions 16
Signs 18
Transportation. General phrases 20
Buying tickets 22
Bus 24
Train 26
On the train. Dialogue (No ticket) 27
Taxi 28
Hotel 30
Restaurant 33
Shopping 35
In town 37
Money 39

Time	41
Greetings. Introductions	43
Farewells	45
Foreign language	47
Apologies	48
Agreement	49
Refusal. Expressing doubt	50
Expressing gratitude	52
Congratulations. Best wishes	53
Socializing	54
Sharing impressions. Emotions	57
Problems. Accidents	59
Health problems	62
At the pharmacy	65
The bare minimum	67

T&P Books Publishing

The bare minimum

Excuse me, …	**Promiňte, …** [promɪnʲtɛ, …]
Hello.	**Dobrý den.** [dobri: dɛn]
Thank you.	**Děkuji.** [dekujɪ]
Good bye.	**Na shledanou.** [na sxlɛdanou]
Yes.	**Ano.** [ano]
No.	**Ne.** [nɛ]
I don't know.	**Nevím.** [nɛvi:m]
Where? | Where to? | When?	**Kde? | Kam? | Kdy?** [gdɛ? | kam? | gdɪ?]

I need …	**Potřebuju …** [potrʒɛbuju …]
I want …	**Chci …** [xtsɪ …]
Do you have …?	**Máte …?** [ma:tɛ …?]
Is there a … here?	**Je tady …?** [jɛ tadɪ …?]
May I …?	**Můžu …?** [mu:ʒu …?]
…, please (polite request)	**…, prosím** […, prosi:m]

I'm looking for …	**Hledám …** [hlɛda:m …]
the restroom	**toaletu** [toalɛtu]
an ATM	**bankomat** [baŋkomat]
a pharmacy (drugstore)	**lékárnu** [lɛ:ka:rnu]
a hospital	**nemocnici** [nɛmotsnɪtsɪ]
the police station	**policejní stanici** [polɪtsɛjni: stanɪtsɪ]
the subway	**metro** [mɛtro]

a taxi	**taxík** [taksi:k]
the train station	**vlakové nádraží** [vlakovɛ na:draʒi:]

My name is …	**Jmenuju se …** [jmɛnuju sɛ …]
What's your name?	**Jak se jmenujete?** [jak sɛ jmɛnujɛtɛ?]
Could you please help me?	**Můžete mi prosím pomoct?** [mu:ʒetɛ mɪ prosi:m pomotst?]
I've got a problem.	**Mám problém.** [ma:m problɛ:m]
I don't feel well.	**Necítím se dobře.** [nɛtsi:ti:m sɛ dobrʒɛ]
Call an ambulance!	**Zavolejte sanitku!** [zavolɛjtɛ sanɪtku!]
May I make a call?	**Můžu si zavolat?** [mu:ʒu sɪ zavolat?]

I'm sorry.	**Omlouvám se.** [omlouva:m sɛ]
You're welcome.	**Není zač.** [nɛni: zatʃ]

I, me	**Já** [ja:]
you (inform.)	**ty** [tɪ]
he	**on** [on]
she	**ona** [ona]
they (masc.)	**oni** [onɪ]
they (fem.)	**ony** [onɪ]
we	**my** [mɪ]
you (pl)	**vy** [vɪ]
you (sg, form.)	**vy** [vɪ]

ENTRANCE	**VCHOD** [vxot]
EXIT	**VÝCHOD** [vi:xot]
OUT OF ORDER	**MIMO PROVOZ** [mɪmo provos]
CLOSED	**ZAVŘENO** [zavrʒɛno]

OPEN	**OTEVŘENO** [otɛvrʒɛno]
FOR WOMEN	**ŽENY** [ʒenɪ]
FOR MEN	**MUŽI** [muʒɪ]

Questions

Where?	**Kde?** [gdɛ?]
Where to?	**Kam?** [kam?]
Where from?	**Odkud?** [otkut?]
Why?	**Proč?** [protʃ?]
For what reason?	**Z jakého důvodu?** [z jakɛːho duːvodu?]
When?	**Kde?** [gdɛ?]
How long?	**Jak dlouho?** [jak dlouho?]
At what time?	**V kolik hodin?** [v kolɪk hodɪn?]
How much?	**Kolik?** [kolɪk?]
Do you have ...?	**Máte ...?** [maːtɛ ...?]
Where is ...?	**Kde je ...?** [gdɛ jɛ ...?]
What time is it?	**Kolik je hodin?** [kolɪk jɛ hodɪn?]
May I make a call?	**Můžu si zavolat?** [muːʒu sɪ zavolat?]
Who's there?	**Kdo je tam?** [gdo jɛ tam?]
Can I smoke here?	**Můžu tady kouřit?** [muːʒu tadɪ kourʒɪt?]
May I ...?	**Můžu ...?** [muːʒu ...?]

Needs

I'd like ...	**Rád /Ráda/ bych ...** [raːd /raːda/ bɪx ...]
I don't want ...	**Nechci ...** [nɛxtsɪ ...]
I'm thirsty.	**Mám žízeň.** [maːm ʒiːzɛnʲ]
I want to sleep.	**Chce se mi spát.** [xtsɛ sɛ mɪ spaːt]

I want ...	**Chci ...** [xtsɪ ...]
to wash up	**se umýt** [sɛ umiːt]
to brush my teeth	**si vyčistit zuby** [sɪ vɪtʃɪstɪt zubɪ]
to rest a while	**si chvilku odpočinout** [sɪ xvɪlku otpotʃɪnout]
to change my clothes	**se převléknout** [sɛ prʒɛvlɛːknout]

to go back to the hotel	**se vrátit do hotelu** [sɛ vraːtɪt do hotɛlu]
to buy ...	**si koupit ...** [sɪ koupɪt ...]
to go to ...	**jít do ...** [jiːt do ...]
to visit ...	**navštívit ...** [navʃtiːvɪt ...]
to meet with ...	**se setkat s ...** [sɛ sɛtkat s ...]
to make a call	**si zavolat** [sɪ zavolat]

I'm tired.	**Jsem unavený /unavená/.** [jsɛm unavɛniː /unavɛnaː/]
We are tired.	**Jsme unavení /unaveny/.** [jsmɛ unavɛniː /unavɛnɪ/]
I'm cold.	**Je mi zima.** [jɛ mɪ zɪma]
I'm hot.	**Je mi horko.** [jɛ mɪ horko]
I'm OK.	**Jsem v pořádku.** [jsɛm v porʒaːtku]

I need to make a call.

Potřebuju si zavolat.
[potrʒɛbuju sɪ zavolat]

I need to go to the restroom.

Potřebuju jít na toaletu.
[potrʒɛbuju jiːt na toalɛtu]

I have to go.

Musím už jít.
[musiːm uʒ jiːt]

I have to go now.

Teď už musím jít.
[tɛtʲ uʒ musiːm jiːt]

Asking for directions

Excuse me, …	**Promiňte, …** [promɪɲɪtɛ, …]
Where is …?	**Kde je …?** [gdɛ jɛ …?]
Which way is …?	**Kudy …?** [kudɪ …?]
Could you help me, please?	**Můžete mi prosím pomoct?** [muːʒɛtɛ mɪ prosiːm pomotst?]

I'm looking for …	**Hledám …** [hlɛdaːm …]
I'm looking for the exit.	**Hledám východ.** [hlɛdaːm viːxot]
I'm going to …	**Jdu …** [jdu …]
Am I going the right way to …?	**Jdu správným směrem do …?** [jdu spraːvniːm smnɛrɛm do …?]

Is it far?	**Je to daleko?** [jɛ to dalɛko?]
Can I get there on foot?	**Dostanu se tam pěšky?** [dostanu sɛ tam pɛʃkɪ?]
Can you show me on the map?	**Můžete mi to ukázat na mapě?** [muːʒɛtɛ mɪ to ukaːzat na mape?]
Show me where we are right now.	**Ukažte mi, kde právě teď jsme.** [ukaʃtɛ mɪ, gdɛ praːvɛ tɛdⁱ jsmɛ]

Here	**Tady** [tadɪ]
There	**Tam** [tam]
This way	**Tudy** [tudɪ]

Turn right.	**Odbočte doprava.** [odbotʃtɛ doprava]
Turn left.	**Odbočte doleva.** [odbotʃtɛ dolɛva]
first (second, third) turn	**první (druhá, třetí) odbočka** [prvni: (druha:, trʒɛti:) odbotʃka]
to the right	**doprava** [doprava]

to the left

doleva
[dolɛva]

Go straight ahead.

Jděte stále rovně.
[jdetɛ sta:lɛ rovne]

Signs

WELCOME!	**VÍTEJTE!** [vi:tɛjtɛ!]
ENTRANCE	**VCHOD** [vxot]
EXIT	**VÝCHOD** [vi:xot]

PUSH	**TLAČIT** [tlatʃɪt]
PULL	**TÁHNOUT** [ta:hnout]
OPEN	**OTEVŘENO** [otɛvrʒɛno]
CLOSED	**ZAVŘENO** [zavrʒɛno]

FOR WOMEN	**ŽENY** [ʒenɪ]
FOR MEN	**MUŽI** [muʒɪ]
GENTLEMEN, GENTS	**PÁNI** [pa:nɪ]
WOMEN	**DÁMY** [da:mɪ]

DISCOUNTS	**VÝPRODEJ** [vi:prodɛj]
SALE	**VÝPRODEJ** [vi:prodɛj]
FREE	**ZDARMA** [zdarma]
NEW!	**NOVINKA!** [novɪŋka!]
ATTENTION!	**POZOR!** [pozor!]

NO VACANCIES	**PLNĚ OBSAZENO** [plne opsazɛno]
RESERVED	**REZERVACE** [rɛzɛrvatsɛ]
ADMINISTRATION	**VEDENÍ** [vɛdɛni:]
STAFF ONLY	**VSTUP JEN PRO ZAMĚSTNANCE** [vstup jɛn pro zamnestnantsɛ]

BEWARE OF THE DOG!	**POZOR PES!** [pozor pɛs!]
NO SMOKING!	**ZÁKAZ KOUŘENÍ** [zaːkaz kourʒɛniː]
DO NOT TOUCH!	**NEDOTÝKEJTE SE** [nɛdotiːkɛjtɛ sɛ]
DANGEROUS	**ŽIVOTU NEBEZPEČNÉ** [ʒɪvotu nɛbɛzpɛtʃnɛː]
DANGER	**NEBEZPEČNÉ** [nɛbɛspɛtʃnɛː]
HIGH VOLTAGE	**VYSOKÉ NAPĚTÍ** [vɪsokɛː napetiː]
NO SWIMMING!	**ZÁKAZ KOUPÁNÍ** [zaːkaz koupaːniː]
OUT OF ORDER	**MIMO PROVOZ** [mɪmo provos]
FLAMMABLE	**HOŘLAVÉ** [horʒlavɛː]
FORBIDDEN	**ZAKÁZÁNO** [zakaːzaːno]
NO TRESPASSING!	**ZÁKAZ VSTUPU** [zaːkaz vstupu]
WET PAINT	**ČERSTVĚ NATŘENO** [tʃerstve natrʃɛno]
CLOSED FOR RENOVATIONS	**UZAVŘENO Z DŮVODU REKONSTRUKCE** [uzavrʒɛno z duːvodu rɛkonstruktsɛ]
WORKS AHEAD	**PRÁCE NA SILNICI** [praːtsɛ na sɪlnɪtsɪ]
DETOUR	**OBJÍŽĎKA** [objiːʒtʲka]

Transportation. General phrases

plane	**letadlo** [lɛtadlo]
train	**vlak** [vlak]
bus	**autobus** [autobus]
ferry	**trajekt** [trajɛkt]
taxi	**taxík** [taksi:k]
car	**auto** [auto]

schedule	**jízdní řád** [ji:zdni: rʒa:t]
Where can I see the schedule?	**Kde se můžu podívat na jízdní řád?** [gdɛ sɛ mu:ʒu podi:vat na ji:zdni: rʒa:t?]
workdays (weekdays)	**pracovní dny** [pratsovni: dnɪ]
weekends	**víkendy** [vi:kɛndɪ]
holidays	**prázdniny** [pra:zdnɪnɪ]

DEPARTURE	**ODJEZD** [odjɛst]
ARRIVAL	**PŘÍJEZD** [prʃi:jɛst]
DELAYED	**ZPOŽDĚNÍ** [zpoʒdeni:]
CANCELLED	**ZRUŠENO** [zruʃeno]

next (train, etc.)	**příští** [prʃi:ʃti:]
first	**první** [prvni:]
last	**poslední** [poslɛdni:]

When is the next ...?	**Kdy jede příští ...?** [gdɪ jɛdɛ prʒi:ʃti: ...?]
When is the first ...?	**Kdy jede první ...?** [gdɪ jɛdɛ prvni: ...?]

When is the last ...?

Kdy jede poslední ...?
[gdɪ jɛdɛ poslɛdni: ...?]

transfer (change of trains, etc.)

přestup
[prʃɛstup]

to make a transfer

přestoupit
[prʃɛstoupɪt]

Do I need to make a transfer?

Musím přestupovat?
[musi:m prʃɛstupovat?]

Buying tickets

Where can I buy tickets?	**Kde si mohu koupit jízdenky?** [gdɛ sɪ mohu koupɪt jiːzdɛŋkɪ?]
ticket	**jízdenka** [jiːzdɛŋka]
to buy a ticket	**koupit si jízdenku** [koupɪt sɪ jiːzdɛŋku]
ticket price	**cena jízdenky** [tsɛna jiːzdɛŋkɪ]

Where to?	**Kam?** [kam?]
To what station?	**Do jaké stanice?** [do jakɛ: stanɪtsɛ?]
I need …	**Potřebuju …** [potrʒɛbuju …]
one ticket	**jednu jízdenku** [jɛdnu jiːzdɛŋku]
two tickets	**dvě jízdenky** [dve jiːzdɛŋkɪ]
three tickets	**tři jízdenky** [trʒɪ jiːzdɛŋkɪ]

one-way	**jízdenka jedním směrem** [jiːzdɛŋka jɛdniːm smnerɛm]
round-trip	**zpáteční jízdenka** [zpaːtɛtʃni: jiːzdɛŋka]
first class	**první třída** [prvni: trʒiːda]
second class	**druhá třída** [druha: trʒiːda]

today	**dnes** [dnɛs]
tomorrow	**zítra** [ziːtra]
the day after tomorrow	**pozítří** [pozi:trʃi:]
in the morning	**dopoledne** [dopolɛdnɛ]
in the afternoon	**odpoledne** [otpolɛdnɛ]
in the evening	**večer** [vɛtʃɛr]

aisle seat

sedadlo u uličky
[sɛdadlo u ulɪtʃkɪ]

window seat

sedadlo u okna
[sɛdadlo u okna]

How much?

Kolik?
[kolɪk?]

Can I pay by credit card?

Můžu platit kreditní kartou?
[muːʒu platɪt krɛdɪtni: kartou?]

Bus

bus	**autobus** [autobus]
intercity bus	**meziměstský autobus** [mɛzɪmnestski: autobus]
bus stop	**autobusová zastávka** [autobusova: zasta:fka]
Where's the nearest bus stop?	**Kde je nejbližší autobusová zastávka?** [gdɛ jɛ nɛjblɪʒʃi: autobusova: zasta:fka?]

number (bus ~, etc.)	**číslo** [tʃi:slo]
Which bus do I take to get to ...?	**Jakým autobusem se dostanu do ...?** [jaki:m autobusɛm sɛ dostanu do ...?]
Does this bus go to ...?	**Jede tento autobus do ...?** [jɛdɛ tɛnto autobus do ...?]
How frequent are the buses?	**Jak často jezdí tento autobus?** [jak tʃasto jɛzdi: tɛnto autobus?]

every 15 minutes	**každých patnáct minut** [kaʒdi:x patna:tst mɪnut]
every half hour	**každou půlhodinu** [kaʒdou pu:lhodɪnu]
every hour	**každou hodinu** [kaʒdou hodɪnu]
several times a day	**několikrát za den** [nekolɪkra:t za dɛn]
... times a day	**... krát za den** [... kra:t za dɛn]

schedule	**jízdní řád** [ji:zdni: rʒa:t]
Where can I see the schedule?	**Kde se můžu podívat na jízdní řád?** [gdɛ sɛ mu:ʒu podi:vat na ji:zdni: rʒa:t?]
When is the next bus?	**Kdy jede příští autobus?** [gdɪ jɛdɛ prʒi:ʃti: autobus?]
When is the first bus?	**Kdy jede první autobus?** [gdɪ jɛdɛ prvni: autobus?]
When is the last bus?	**Kdy jede poslední autobus?** [gdɪ jɛdɛ poslɛdni: autobus?]

stop	**zastávka** [zasta:fka]
next stop	**příští zastávka** [prʃi:ʃti: zasta:fka]

last stop (terminus)	**poslední zastávka** [poslɛdni: zasta:fka]
Stop here, please.	**Zastavte tady, prosím.** [zastaftɛ tadɪ, prosi:m]
Excuse me, this is my stop.	**Promiňte, já tady vystupuju.** [promɪnˈtɛ, ja: tadɪ vɪstupuju]

Train

train	**vlak** [vlak]
suburban train	**příměstský vlak** [prʒi:mnestskɪ vlak]
long-distance train	**dálkový vlak** [da:lkovi: vlak]
train station	**vlakové nádraží** [vlakovɛ: na:draʒi:]
Excuse me, where is the exit to the platform?	**Promiňte, kde je vstup na nástupiště?** [promɪɲtɛ, gdɛ jɛ vstup na na:stupɪʃte?]
Does this train go to ...?	**Jede tento vlak do ...?** [jɛdɛ tɛnto vlak do ...?]
next train	**příští vlak** [prʃi:ʃti: vlak]
When is the next train?	**Kdy jede příští vlak?** [gdɪ jɛdɛ prʒi:ʃti: vlak?]
Where can I see the schedule?	**Kde se můžu podívat na jízdní řád?** [gdɛ sɛ mu:ʒu podi:vat na ji:zdnɪ: rʒa:t?]
From which platform?	**Ze kterého nástupiště?** [zɛ ktɛrɛ:ho na:stupɪʃte?]
When does the train arrive in ...?	**Kdy přijede tento vlak do ...?** [gdɪ prʃɪjɛdɛ tɛnto vlak do ...?]
Please help me.	**Můžete mi prosím pomoct?** [mu:ʒetɛ mɪ prosi:m pomotst?]
I'm looking for my seat.	**Hledám své místo.** [hlɛda:m svɛ: mi:sto]
We're looking for our seats.	**Hledáme svá místa.** [hlɛda:mɛ sva: mi:sta]
My seat is taken.	**Moje místo je obsazeno.** [mojɛ mi:sto jɛ opsazɛno]
Our seats are taken.	**Naše místa jsou obsazena.** [naʃɛ mi:sta jsou opsazɛna]
I'm sorry but this is my seat.	**Promiňte, ale toto je moje místo.** [promɪɲtɛ, alɛ toto jɛ mojɛ mi:sto]
Is this seat taken?	**Je toto místo volné?** [jɛ toto mi:sto volnɛ:?]
May I sit here?	**Můžu si zde sednout?** [mu:ʒu sɪ zdɛ sɛdnout?]

On the train. Dialogue (No ticket)

Ticket, please.	**Jízdenku, prosím.** [ji:zdɛŋku, prosi:m]
I don't have a ticket.	**Nemám jízdenku.** [nɛma:m ji:zdɛŋku]
I lost my ticket.	**Ztratil jsem jízdenku.** [stratɪl jsɛm ji:zdɛŋku]
I forgot my ticket at home.	**Zapomněl svou jízdenku doma.** [zapomel svou ji:zdɛŋku doma]

You can buy a ticket from me.	**Jízdenku si můžete koupit u mě.** [ji:zdɛŋku sɪ mu:ʒetɛ koupɪt u mne]
You will also have to pay a fine.	**Také budete muset zaplatit pokutu.** [takɛ: budɛtɛ musɛt zaplatɪt pokutu]
Okay.	**Dobrá.** [dobra:]
Where are you going?	**Kam jedete?** [kam jɛdɛtɛ?]
I'm going to ...	**Jedu do ...** [jɛdu do ...]

How much? I don't understand.	**Kolik? Nerozumím.** [kolɪk? nɛrozumi:m]
Write it down, please.	**Napište to, prosím.** [napɪʃtɛ to, prosi:m]
Okay. Can I pay with a credit card?	**Dobrá. Můžu platit kreditní kartou?** [dobra:. mu:ʒu platɪt krɛdɪtni: kartou?]
Yes, you can.	**Ano, můžete.** [ano, mu:ʒetɛ]

Here's your receipt.	**Tady je vaše stvrzenka.** [tadɪ jɛ vaʃɛ stvrzɛŋka]
Sorry about the fine.	**Omlouvám se za tu pokutu.** [omlouva:m sɛ za tu pokutu]
That's okay. It was my fault.	**To je v pořádku. Je to moje chyba.** [to jɛ v porʒa:tku. jɛ to mojɛ xɪba]
Enjoy your trip.	**Příjemnou cestu.** [prʒi:jɛmnou tsɛstu]

Taxi

taxi	**taxík** [taksi:k]
taxi driver	**taxikář** [taksɪka:rʒ]
to catch a taxi	**chytit si taxík** [xɪtɪt sɪ taksi:k]
taxi stand	**stanoviště taxíků** [stanovɪʃte taksi:ku:]
Where can I get a taxi?	**Kde můžu sehnat taxík?** [gdɛ mu:ʒu sɛhnat taksi:k?]

to call a taxi	**volat taxík** [volat taksi:k]
I need a taxi.	**Potřebuju taxík.** [potrʒɛbuju taksi:k]
Right now.	**Hned teď.** [hnɛt tɛtʲ]
What is your address (location)?	**Jaká je vaše adresa?** [jaka: jɛ vaʃɛ adrɛsa?]
My address is ...	**Moje adresa je ...** [mojɛ adrɛsa jɛ ...]
Your destination?	**Váš cíl?** [va:ʃ tsi:l?]
Excuse me, ...	**Promiňte, ...** [promɪnʲtɛ, ...]
Are you available?	**Jste volný?** [jstɛ volni:?]
How much is it to get to ...?	**Kolik to stojí do ...?** [kolɪk to stoji: do ...?]
Do you know where it is?	**Víte, kde to je?** [vi:tɛ, gdɛ to jɛ?]

Airport, please.	**Na letiště, prosím.** [na lɛtɪʃte, prosi:m]
Stop here, please.	**Zastavte tady, prosím.** [zastaftɛ tadɪ, prosi:m]
It's not here.	**To není tady.** [to nɛni: tadɪ]
This is the wrong address.	**To je nesprávná adresa.** [to jɛ nɛspra:vna: adrɛsa]
Turn left.	**Zabočte doleva.** [zabotʃtɛ dolɛva]
Turn right.	**Zabočte doprava.** [zabotʃtɛ doprava]

How much do I owe you?

Kolik vám dlužím?
[kolɪk va:m dluʒi:m?]

I'd like a receipt, please.

Chtěl /Chtěla/ bych stvrzenku, prosím.
[xtel /xtela/ bɪx stvrzɛŋku, prosi:m]

Keep the change.

Drobné si nechte.
[drobnɛ: sɪ nɛxtɛ]

Would you please wait for me?

Můžete tady na mě počkat?
[mu:ʒetɛ tadɪ na mne potʃkat?]

five minutes

pět minut
[pet mɪnut]

ten minutes

deset minut
[dɛsɛt mɪnut]

fifteen minutes

patnáct minut
[patna:tst mɪnut]

twenty minutes

dvacet minut
[dvatsɛt mɪnut]

half an hour

půl hodiny
[pu:l hodɪnɪ]

Hotel

Hello.	**Dobrý den.** [dobri: dɛn]
My name is ...	**Jmenuju se ...** [jmɛnuju sɛ ...]
I have a reservation.	**Mám tady rezervaci.** [ma:m tadɪ rɛzɛrvatsɪ]

I need ...	**Potřebuju ...** [potrʒɛbuju ...]
a single room	**jednolůžkový pokoj** [jɛdnolu:ʃkovi: pokoj]
a double room	**dvoulůžkový pokoj** [dvoulu:ʃkovi: pokoj]
How much is that?	**Kolik to stojí?** [kolɪk to stoji:?]
That's a bit expensive.	**To je trochu drahé.** [to jɛ troxu drahɛ:]

Do you have anything else?	**Máte nějaké další možnosti?** [ma:tɛ nejakɛ: dalʃi: moʒnostɪ?]
I'll take it.	**To si vezmu.** [to sɪ vɛzmu]
I'll pay in cash.	**Budu platit v hotovosti.** [budu platɪt v hotovostɪ]

I've got a problem.	**Mám problém.** [ma:m problɛ:m]
My ... is broken.	**... je rozbitý /rozbitá/.** [... jɛ rozbɪti: /rozbɪta:/]
My ... is out of order.	**... je mimo provoz.** [... jɛ mɪmo provoz]
TV	**Můj televizor ...** [mu:j tɛlɛvɪzor ...]
air conditioner	**Moje klimatizace ...** [mojɛ klɪmatɪzatsɛ ...]
tap	**Můj kohoutek ...** [mu:j kohoutɛk ...]

shower	**Moje sprcha ...** [mojɛ sprxa ...]
sink	**Můj dřez ...** [mu:j drʒɛz ...]
safe	**Můj sejf ...** [mu:j sɛjf ...]

door lock	**Můj zámek ...** [mu:j za:mɛk ...]
electrical outlet	**Moje elektrická zásuvka ...** [mojɛ ɛlɛktrɪtska: za:sufka ...]
hairdryer	**Můj fén ...** [mu:j fɛ:n ...]

I don't have ...	**Nemám ...** [nɛma:m ...]
water	**vodu** [vodu]
light	**světlo** [svetlo]
electricity	**elektřinu** [ɛlɛktrʒɪnu]

Can you give me ...?	**Můžete mi dát ...?** [mu:ʒetɛ mɪ da:t ...?]
a towel	**ručník** [rutʃni:k]
a blanket	**přikrývku** [prʒɪkri:fku]
slippers	**bačkory** [batʃkorɪ]
a robe	**župan** [ʒupan]
shampoo	**šampón** [ʃampón]
soap	**mýdlo** [mi:dlo]

I'd like to change rooms.	**Chtěl bych vyměnit pokoje.** [xtel bɪx vɪmnenɪt pokojɛ]
I can't find my key.	**Nemůžu najít klíč.** [nɛmu:ʒu naji:t kli:tʃ]
Could you open my room, please?	**Můžete mi otevřít pokoj, prosím?** [mu:ʒetɛ mɪ otɛvrʒi:t pokoj, prosi:m?]
Who's there?	**Kdo je tam?** [gdo jɛ tam?]
Come in!	**Vstupte!** [vstuptɛ!]
Just a minute!	**Minutku!** [mɪnutku!]
Not right now, please.	**Teď ne, prosím.** [tɛtⁱ nɛ, prosi:m]

Come to my room, please.	**Pojďte do mého pokoje, prosím.** [pojdⁱtɛ do mɛ:ho pokojɛ, prosi:m]
I'd like to order food service.	**Chtěl bych si objednat jídlo.** [xtel bɪx sɪ objɛdnat ji:dlo]
My room number is ...	**Číslo mého pokoje je ...** [tʃi:slo mɛ:ho pokojɛ jɛ ...]

I'm leaving …	**Odjíždím …** [odjiːʒdiːm …]
We're leaving …	**Odjíždíme …** [odjiːʒdiːmɛ …]
right now	**hned teď** [hnɛt tɛtʲ]
this afternoon	**dnes odpoledne** [dnɛs otpolɛdnɛ]
tonight	**dnes večer** [dnɛs vɛtʃɛr]
tomorrow	**zítra** [ziːtra]
tomorrow morning	**zítra dopoledne** [ziːtra dopolɛdnɛ]
tomorrow evening	**zítra večer** [ziːtra vɛtʃɛr]
the day after tomorrow	**pozítří** [poziːtrʃiː]

I'd like to pay.	**Chtěl bych zaplatit.** [xtel bɪx zaplatɪt]
Everything was wonderful.	**Všechno bylo skvělé.** [vʃɛxno bɪlo skvelɛː]
Where can I get a taxi?	**Kde můžu sehnat taxík?** [gdɛ muːʒu sɛhnat taksiːk?]
Would you call a taxi for me, please?	**Můžete mi zavolat taxík, prosím?** [muːʒetɛ mɪ zavolat taksiːk, prosiːm?]

Restaurant

Can I look at the menu, please?	**Můžu se podívat na jídelní lístek, prosím?** [muːʒu sɛ podiːvat na jiːdɛlniː liːstɛk, prosiːm?]
Table for one.	**Stůl pro jednoho.** [stuːl pro jɛdnoho]
There are two (three, four) of us.	**Jsme dva (tři, čtyři).** [jsmɛ dva (trʒɪ, tʃtɪrʒɪ)]
Smoking	**Kuřáci** [kurʒaːtsɪ]
No smoking	**Nekuřáci** [nɛkurʒaːtsɪ]
Excuse me! (addressing a waiter)	**Promiňte!** [promɪnʲtɛ!]
menu	**jídelní lístek** [jiːdɛlniː liːstɛk]
wine list	**vinný lístek** [vɪnniː liːstɛk]
The menu, please.	**Jídelní lístek, prosím.** [jiːdɛlniː liːstɛk, prosiːm]
Are you ready to order?	**Vybrali jste si?** [vɪbralɪ jstɛ sɪ?]
What will you have?	**Co si dáte?** [tso sɪ daːtɛ?]
I'll have ...	**Dám si ...** [daːm sɪ ...]
I'm a vegetarian.	**Jsem vegetarián.** [jsɛm vɛgɛtariaːn]
meat	**maso** [maso]
fish	**ryba** [rɪba]
vegetables	**zelenina** [zɛlɛnɪna]
Do you have vegetarian dishes?	**Máte vegetariánská jídla?** [maːtɛ vɛgɛtariaːnskaː jiːdla?]
I don't eat pork.	**Nejím vepřové.** [nɛjiːm vɛprʃovɛː]
Band-Aid	**On /ona/ nejí maso.** [on /ona/ nɛjiː maso]
I am allergic to ...	**Jsem alergický /alergická/ na ...** [jsɛm alɛrgɪtski: /alɛrgɪtskaː/ na ...]

Would you please bring me ...

Přinesl byste mi prosím ...
[prʒɪnɛsl bɪstɛ mɪ prosi:m ...]

salt | pepper | sugar

sůl | pepř | cukr
[su:l | pɛprʒ | tsukr]

coffee | tea | dessert

kávu | čaj | zákusek
[ka:vu | tʃaj | za:kusɛk]

water | sparkling | plain

vodu | perlivou | neperlivou
[vodu | pɛrlɪvou | nɛpɛrlɪvou]

a spoon | fork | knife

lžíci | vidličku | nůž
[lʒi:tsɪ | vɪdlɪtʃku | nu:ʒ]

a plate | napkin

talíř | ubrousek
[tali:rʒ | ubrousɛk]

Enjoy your meal!

Dobrou chuť!
[dobrou xutʲl]

One more, please.

Ještě jednou, prosím.
[jɛʃte jɛdnou, prosi:m]

It was very delicious.

Bylo to výborné.
[bɪlo to vi:bornɛ:]

check | change | tip

účet | drobné | spropitné
[u:tʃɛt | drobnɛ: | spropɪtnɛ:]

Check, please.
(Could I have the check, please?)

Účet, prosím.
[u:tʃɛt, prosi:m]

Can I pay by credit card?

Můžu platit kreditní kartou?
[mu:ʒu platɪt krɛdɪtni: kartou?]

I'm sorry, there's a mistake here.

Omlouvám se, ale tady je chyba.
[omlouva:m sɛ, alɛ tadɪ jɛ xɪba]

Shopping

Can I help you?	**Co si přejete?** [tso sɪ prʒɛjɛtɛ?]
Do you have …?	**Máte …?** [ma:tɛ …?]
I'm looking for …	**Hledám …** [hlɛda:m …]
I need …	**Potřebuju …** [potrʒɛbuju …]

I'm just looking.	**Jen se dívám.** [jɛn sɛ di:va:m]
We're just looking.	**Jen se díváme.** [jɛn sɛ di:va:mɛ]
I'll come back later.	**Vrátím se později.** [vra:ti:m sɛ pozdejɪ]
We'll come back later.	**Vrátíme se později.** [vra:ti:mɛ sɛ pozdejɪ]
discounts | sale	**slevy | výprodej** [slɛvɪ | vi:prodɛj]

Would you please show me …	**Můžete mi prosím ukázat …** [mu:ʒetɛ mɪ prosi:m uka:zat …]
Would you please give me …	**Můžete mi prosím dát …** [mu:ʒetɛ mɪ prosi:m da:t …]
Can I try it on?	**Můžu si to vyzkoušet?** [mu:ʒu sɪ to vɪskoufɛt?]
Excuse me, where's the fitting room?	**Promiňte, kde je zkušební kabinka?** [promɪɲtɛ, gdɛ jɛ skufɛbni: kabɪŋka?]
Which color would you like?	**Jakou byste chtěl /chtěla/ barvu?** [jakou bɪstɛ xtel /xtela/ barvu?]
size | length	**velikost | délku** [vɛlɪkost | dɛ:lku]
How does it fit?	**Jak vám to sedí?** [jak va:m to sɛdi:?]

How much is it?	**Kolik to stojí?** [kolɪk to stoji:?]
That's too expensive.	**To je příliš drahé.** [to jɛ prfi:lɪf drahɛ:]
I'll take it.	**Vezmu si to.** [vɛzmu sɪ to]
Excuse me, where do I pay?	**Promiňte, kde můžu zaplatit?** [promɪɲtɛ, gdɛ mu:ʒu zaplatɪt?]

Will you pay in cash or credit card?	**Budete platit v hotovosti nebo kreditní kartou?** [budɛtɛ platɪt v hotovostɪ nɛbo krɛdɪtni: kartou?]
In cash | with credit card	**v hotovosti | kreditní kartou** [v hotovostɪ | krɛdɪtni: kartou]

Do you want the receipt?	**Chcete stvrzenku?** [xtsɛtɛ stvrzɛŋku?]
Yes, please.	**Ano, prosím.** [ano, prosi:m]
No, it's OK.	**Ne, to je dobré.** [nɛ, to jɛ dobrɛ:]
Thank you. Have a nice day!	**Děkuji. Hezký den.** [dɛkujɪ. hɛski: dɛn]

In town

Excuse me, ...	**Promiňte, prosím.** [promɪnʲtɛ, prosiːm]
I'm looking for ...	**Hledám ...** [hlɛdaːm ...]
the subway	**metro** [mɛtro]
my hotel	**svůj hotel** [svuːj hotɛl]
the movie theater	**kino** [kɪno]
a taxi stand	**stanoviště taxíků** [stanovɪʃtɛ taksiːkuː]

an ATM	**bankomat** [baŋkomat]
a foreign exchange office	**směnárnu** [smnenaːrnu]
an internet café	**internetovou kavárnu** [ɪntɛrnɛtovou kavaːrnu]
... street	**... ulici** [... ulɪtsɪ]
this place	**toto místo** [toto miːsto]

Do you know where ... is?	**Nevíte, kde je ...?** [nɛviːtɛ, gdɛ jɛ ...?]
Which street is this?	**Jaká je toto ulice?** [jaka: jɛ toto ulɪtsɛ?]
Show me where we are right now.	**Ukažte mi, kde teď jsme.** [ukaʃtɛ mɪ, gdɛ tɛdʲ jsmɛ]
Can I get there on foot?	**Dostanu se tam pěšky?** [dostanu sɛ tam pɛʃkɪ?]
Do you have a map of the city?	**Máte mapu tohoto města?** [maːtɛ mapu tohoto mnesta?]

How much is a ticket to get in?	**Kolik stojí vstupenka?** [kolɪk stojiː vstupɛŋka?]
Can I take pictures here?	**Můžu tady fotit?** [muːʒu tadɪ fotɪt?]
Are you open?	**Máte otevřeno?** [maːtɛ otɛvrʒɛno?]

When do you open?	**Kdy otvíráte?**
	[gdɪ otviːraːtɛ?]
When do you close?	**Kdy zavíráte?**
	[gdɪ zaviːraːtɛ?]

Money

money	**peníze** [pɛniːzɛ]
cash	**hotovost** [hotovost]
paper money	**papírové peníze** [papiːrovɛ pɛniːzɛ]
loose change	**drobné** [drobnɛː]
check | change | tip	**účet | drobné | spropitné** [uːt͡ʃɛt | drobnɛː | spropɪtnɛː]

credit card	**kreditní karta** [krɛdɪtniː karta]
wallet	**peněženka** [pɛnɛʒɛŋka]
to buy	**koupit** [koupɪt]
to pay	**platit** [platɪt]
fine	**pokuta** [pokuta]
free	**zdarma** [zdarma]

Where can I buy ...?	**Kde dostanu koupit ...?** [gdɛ dostanu koupɪt ...?]
Is the bank open now?	**Je teď otevřená banka?** [jɛ tɛdʲ otɛvrʒɛnaː baŋka?]
When does it open?	**Kdy otvírají?** [gdɪ otviːrajiː?]
When does it close?	**Kdy zavírají?** [gdɪ zaviːrajiː?]

How much?	**Kolik?** [kolɪk?]
How much is this?	**Kolik to stojí?** [kolɪk to stojiː?]
That's too expensive.	**To je příliš drahé.** [to jɛ prʃiːlɪʃ drahɛː]

Excuse me, where do I pay?	**Promiňte, kde můžu zaplatit?** [promɪɲʲtɛ, gdɛ muːʒu zaplatɪt?]
Check, please.	**Účet, prosím.** [uːt͡ʃɛt, prosiːm]

Can I pay by credit card?

Můžu platit kreditní kartou?
[muːʒu platɪt krɛdɪtniː kartou?]

Is there an ATM here?

Je tady bankomat?
[jɛ tadɪ baŋkomat?]

I'm looking for an ATM.

Hledám bankomat.
[hlɛdaːm baŋkomat]

I'm looking for a foreign exchange office.

Hledám směnárnu.
[hlɛdaːm smnenaːrnu]

I'd like to change ...

Chtěl bych si vyměnit ...
[xtel bɪx sɪ vɪmnenɪt ...]

What is the exchange rate?

Jaký je kurz?
[jakiː jɛ kurs?]

Do you need my passport?

Potřebujete můj pas?
[potrʒɛbujɛtɛ muːj pas?]

Time

What time is it?	**Kolik je hodin?** [kolɪk jɛ hodɪn?]
When?	**Kdy?** [gdɪ?]
At what time?	**V kolik hodin?** [v kolɪk hodɪn?]
now | later | after …	**teď | později | po …** [tɛdʲ | pozdejɪ | po …]
one o'clock	**jedna hodina** [jɛdna hodɪna]
one fifteen	**čtvrt na dvě** [tʃtvrt na dve]
one thirty	**půl druhé** [puːl druhɛː]
one forty-five	**tři čtvrtě na dvě** [trʒɪ tʃtvrte na dve]
one | two | three	**jedna | dvě | tři** [jɛdna | dve | trʒɪ]
four | five | six	**čtyři | pět | šest** [tʃtɪrʒɪ | pet | ʃɛst]
seven | eight | nine	**sedm | osm | devět** [sɛdm | osm | dɛvet]
ten | eleven | twelve	**deset | jedenáct | dvanáct** [dɛsɛt | jɛdɛnaːtst | dvanaːtst]
in …	**za …** [za …]
five minutes	**pět minut** [pet mɪnut]
ten minutes	**deset minut** [dɛsɛt mɪnut]
fifteen minutes	**patnáct minut** [patnaːtst mɪnut]
twenty minutes	**dvacet minut** [dvatsɛt mɪnut]
half an hour	**půl hodiny** [puːl hodɪnɪ]
an hour	**hodinu** [hodɪnu]

in the morning	**dopoledne** [dopolɛdnɛ]
early in the morning	**brzy ráno** [brzɪ ra:no]
this morning	**dnes dopoledne** [dnɛs dopolɛdnɛ]
tomorrow morning	**zítra dopoledne** [zi:tra dopolɛdnɛ]
in the middle of the day	**v poledne** [v polɛdnɛ]
in the afternoon	**odpoledne** [otpolɛdnɛ]
in the evening	**večer** [vɛtʃɛr]
tonight	**dnes večer** [dnɛs vɛtʃɛr]
at night	**v noci** [v notsɪ]
yesterday	**včera** [vtʃɛra]
today	**dnes** [dnɛs]
tomorrow	**zítra** [zi:tra]
the day after tomorrow	**pozítří** [pozi:trʃi:]
What day is it today?	**Kolikátého je dnes?** [kolɪka:tɛ:ho jɛ dnɛs?]
It's ...	**Dnes je ...** [dnɛs jɛ ...]
Monday	**pondělí** [pondeli:]
Tuesday	**úterý** [u:tɛri:]
Wednesday	**středa** [strʒɛda]
Thursday	**čtvrtek** [tʃtvrtɛk]
Friday	**pátek** [pa:tɛk]
Saturday	**sobota** [sobota]
Sunday	**neděle** [nɛdelɛ]

Greetings. Introductions

Hello.	**Dobrý den.** [dobri: dɛn]
Pleased to meet you.	**Těší mě, že vás poznávám.** [teʃi: mne, ʒe va:s pozna:va:m]
Me too.	**Mě také.** [mne takɛ:]
I'd like you to meet …	**Rád /Ráda/ bych** **vás seznámil /seznámila/ …** [ra:d /ra:da/ bɪx va:s sɛzna:mɪl /sɛzna:mɪla/ …]
Nice to meet you.	**Těší mě.** [teʃi: mne]
How are you?	**Jak se máte?** [jak sɛ ma:tɛ?]
My name is …	**Jmenuju se …** [jmɛnuju sɛ …]
His name is …	**On se jmenuje …** [on sɛ jmɛnujɛ …]
Her name is …	**Ona se jmenuje …** [ona sɛ jmɛnujɛ …]
What's your name?	**Jak se jmenujete?** [jak sɛ jmɛnujɛtɛ?]
What's his name?	**Jak se jmenuje?** [jak sɛ jmɛnujɛ?]
What's her name?	**Jak se jmenuje?** [jak sɛ jmɛnujɛ?]
What's your last name?	**Jaké je vaše příjmení?** [jakɛ: jɛ vaʃe prʒi:jmɛni:?]
You can call me …	**Můžete mi říkat …** [mu:ʒetɛ mɪ rʒi:kat …]
Where are you from?	**Odkud jste?** [otkut jstɛ?]
I'm from …	**Jsem z …** [jsɛm s …]
What do you do for a living?	**Čím jste?** [tʃi:m jstɛ?]
Who is this?	**Kdo to je?** [gdo to jɛ?]
Who is he?	**Kdo je on?** [gdo jɛ on?]

Who is she?	**Kdo je ona?** [gdo jɛ ona?]
Who are they?	**Kdo jsou oni?** [gdo jsou onɪ?]

This is ...	**To je ...** [to jɛ ...]
my friend (masc.)	**můj přítel** [muːj prʃiːtɛl]
my friend (fem.)	**moje přítelkyně** [mojɛ prʃiːtɛlkɪne]
my husband	**můj manžel** [muːj manʒel]
my wife	**moje manželka** [mojɛ manʒelka]

my father	**můj otec** [muːj otɛts]
my mother	**moje matka** [mojɛ matka]
my brother	**můj bratr** [muːj bratr]
my sister	**moje sestra** [mojɛ sɛstra]
my son	**můj syn** [muːj sɪn]
my daughter	**moje dcera** [mojɛ dtsɛra]

This is our son.	**To je náš syn.** [to jɛ naːʃ sɪn]
This is our daughter.	**To je naše dcera.** [to jɛ naʃɛ dtsɛra]
These are my children.	**To jsou moje děti.** [to jsou mojɛ detɪ]
These are our children.	**To jsou naše děti.** [to jsou naʃɛ detɪ]

Farewells

Good bye!	**Na shledanou!** [na sxlɛdanou!]
Bye! (inform.)	**Ahoj!** [ahoj!]
See you tomorrow.	**Uvidíme se zítra.** [uvɪdiːmɛ sɛ ziːtra]
See you soon.	**Brzy ahoj.** [brzɪ ahoj]
See you at seven.	**Ahoj v sedm.** [ahoj v sɛdm]
Have fun!	**Hezkou zábavu!** [hɛskou zaːbavu!]
Talk to you later.	**Promluvíme si později.** [promluviːmɛ sɪ pozdejɪ]
Have a nice weekend.	**Hezký víkend.** [hɛskɪ viːkɛnt]
Good night.	**Dobrou noc.** [dobrou nots]
It's time for me to go.	**Už musím jít.** [uʒ musiːm jiːt]
I have to go.	**Musím jít.** [musiːm jiːt]
I will be right back.	**Hned se vrátím.** [hnɛt sɛ vraːtiːm]
It's late.	**Je pozdě.** [jɛ pozde]
I have to get up early.	**Musím brzy vstávat.** [musiːm brzɪ vstaːvat]
I'm leaving tomorrow.	**Zítra odjíždím.** [ziːtra odjiːʒdiːm]
We're leaving tomorrow.	**Zítra odjíždíme.** [ziːtra odjiːʒdiːmɛ]
Have a nice trip!	**Hezký výlet!** [hɛskɪ vɪlɛt!]
It was nice meeting you.	**Jsem rád /ráda/,** **že jsem vás poznal /poznala/.** [jsɛm raːd /raːda/, ʒe jsɛm vaːs poznal /poznala/]

It was nice talking to you.

Rád /Ráda/ jsem si s vámi popovídal /popovídala/.
[ra:d /ra:da/ jsɛm sɪ s va:mɪ popoviːdal /popoviːdala/]

Thanks for everything.

Děkuji vám za všechno.
[dekujɪ va:m za vʃɛxno]

I had a very good time.

Měl /Měla/ jsem se moc dobře.
[mnel /mnela/ jsɛm sɛ mots dobrʒɛ]

We had a very good time.

Měli /Měly/ jsme se moc dobře.
[mnelɪ /mnelɪ/ jsmɛ sɛ mots dobrʒɛ]

It was really great.

Bylo to fakt skvělé.
[bɪlo to fakt skvelɛ:]

I'm going to miss you.

Bude se mi po tobě stýskat.
[budɛ sɛ mɪ po tobe sti:skat]

We're going to miss you.

Bude se nám po vás stýskat.
[budɛ sɛ na:m po va:s sti:skat]

Good luck!

Hodně štěstí!
[hodne ʃtesti:!]

Say hi to ...

Pozdravuj ...
[pozdravuj ...]

Foreign language

I don't understand.	**Nerozumím.** [nɛrozumiːm]
Write it down, please.	**Napište to, prosím.** [napɪʃtɛ to, prosiːm]
Do you speak …?	**Mluvíte …?** [mluviːtɛ …?]

I speak a little bit of …	**Mluvím trochu …** [mluviːm troxu …]
English	**anglicky** [anglɪtskɪ]
Turkish	**turecky** [turɛtskɪ]
Arabic	**arabsky** [arapskɪ]
French	**francouzsky** [frantsouskɪ]

German	**německy** [nemɛtskɪ]
Italian	**italsky** [ɪtalskɪ]
Spanish	**španělsky** [ʃpanelskɪ]
Portuguese	**portugalsky** [portugalskɪ]
Chinese	**čínsky** [tʃiːnskɪ]
Japanese	**japonsky** [japonskɪ]

Can you repeat that, please.	**Můžete to prosím zopakovat.** [muːʒɛtɛ to prosiːm zopakovat]
I understand.	**Rozumím.** [rozumiːm]
I don't understand.	**Nerozumím.** [nɛrozumiːm]
Please speak more slowly.	**Mluvte prosím pomalu.** [mluftɛ prosiːm pomalu]

Is that correct? (Am I saying it right?)	**Je to správně?** [jɛ to spraːvne?]
What is this? (What does this mean?)	**Co to je?** [tso to jɛ?]

Apologies

Excuse me, please.	**Promiňte, prosím.** [promɪnʲtɛ, prosiːm]
I'm sorry.	**Omlouvám se.** [omlouvaːm sɛ]
I'm really sorry.	**Je mi to opravdu líto.** [jɛ mɪ to opravdu liːto]
Sorry, it's my fault.	**Omlouvám se, je to moje chyba.** [omlouvaːm sɛ, jɛ to mojɛ xɪba]
My mistake.	**Moje chyba.** [mojɛ xɪba]

May I ...?	**Můžu ...?** [muːʒu ...?]
Do you mind if I ...?	**Nevadilo by vám, kdybych ...?** [nɛvadɪlo bɪ vaːm, gdɪbɪx ...?]
It's OK.	**Nic se nestalo.** [nɪts sɛ nɛstalo]
It's all right.	**To je v pořádku.** [to jɛ v porʒaːtku]
Don't worry about it.	**Tím se netrapte.** [tiːm sɛ nɛtraptɛ]

Agreement

Yes. **Ano.**
[ano]

Yes, sure. **Ano, jistě.**
[ano, jɪste]

OK (Good!) **Dobrá.**
[dobra:]

Very well. **Dobře.**
[dobrʒɛ]

Certainly! **Samozřejmě!**
[samozrʒɛjmne!]

I agree. **Souhlasím.**
[souhlasi:m]

That's correct. **To je správně.**
[to jɛ spra:vne]

That's right. **To je v pořádku.**
[to jɛ v porʒa:tku]

You're right. **Máte pravdu.**
[ma:tɛ pravdu]

I don't mind. **Nevadí mi to.**
[nɛvadi: mɪ to]

Absolutely right. **To je naprosto správně.**
[to jɛ naprosto spra:vne]

It's possible. **Je to možné.**
[jɛ to moʒnɛ:]

That's a good idea. **To je dobrý nápad.**
[to jɛ dobri: na:pat]

I can't say no. **Nemůžu říct ne.**
[nɛmu:ʒu rʒi:tst nɛ]

I'd be happy to. **Hrozně rád /ráda/.**
[hrozne ra:d /ra:da/]

With pleasure. **S radostí.**
[s radosti:]

Refusal. Expressing doubt

No. **Ne.**
[nɛ]

Certainly not. **Určitě ne.**
[urtʃɪtɛ nɛ]

I don't agree. **Nesouhlasím.**
[nɛsouhlasi:m]

I don't think so. **Myslím, že ne.**
[mɪsli:m, ʒe nɛ]

It's not true. **To není pravda.**
[to nɛni: pravda]

You are wrong. **Mýlíte se.**
[mɪli:tɛ sɛ]

I think you are wrong. **Myslím, že se mýlíte.**
[mɪsli:m, ʒe sɛ mi:li:tɛ]

I'm not sure. **Nejsem si jist /jista/.**
[nɛjsɛm sɪ jɪst /jɪsta/]

It's impossible. **To je nemožné.**
[to jɛ nɛmoʒnɛ:]

Nothing of the kind (sort)! **Nic takového!**
[nɪts takovɛ:ho!]

The exact opposite. **Přesně naopak.**
[prʃɛsne naopak]

I'm against it. **Jsem proti.**
[jsɛm protɪ]

I don't care. **Je mi to jedno.**
[jɛ mɪ to jɛdno]

I have no idea. **Nemám ani ponětí.**
[nɛma:m anɪ poneti:]

I doubt it. **To pochybuju.**
[to poxɪbuju]

Sorry, I can't. **Bohužel, nemůžu.**
[bohuʒel, nɛmu:ʒu]

Sorry, I don't want to. **Bohužel, nechci.**
[bohuʒel, nɛxtsɪ]

Thank you, but I don't need this. **Děkuju, ale to já nepotřebuju.**
[dekuju, alɛ to ja: nɛpotrʒɛbuju]

It's getting late. **Už je pozdě.**
[uʒ jɛ pozde]

I have to get up early.

Musím brzy vstávat.
[musiːm brzɪ vstaːvat]

I don't feel well.

Necítím se dobře.
[nɛtsiːtiːm sɛ dobrʒɛ]

Expressing gratitude

Thank you.	**Děkuju.** [dekuju]
Thank you very much.	**Děkuju mockrát.** [dekuju motskra:t]
I really appreciate it.	**Opravdu si toho vážím.** [opravdu sɪ toho va:ʒi:m]
I'm really grateful to you.	**Jsem vám opravdu vděčný /vděčná/.** [jsɛm va:m opravdu vdetʃni: /vdetʃna:/]
We are really grateful to you.	**Jsme vám opravdu vděční.** [jsmɛ va:m opravdu vdetʃni:]

Thank you for your time.	**Děkuju za váš čas.** [dekuju za va:ʃ tʃas]
Thanks for everything.	**Děkuju za všechno.** [dekuju za vʃexno]
Thank you for ...	**Děkuju za ...** [dekuju za ...]
your help	**vaši pomoc** [vaʃɪ pomots]
a nice time	**příjemně strávený čas** [prʒi:jɛme stra:vɛnɪ tʃas]

a wonderful meal	**skvělé jídlo** [skvelɛ: ji:dlo]
a pleasant evening	**příjemný večer** [prʒi:jɛmnɪ vɛtʃɛr]
a wonderful day	**nádherný den** [na:dhɛrni: dɛn]
an amazing journey	**úžasnou cestu** [u:ʒasnou tsɛstu]

Don't mention it.	**To nestojí za řeč.** [to nɛstoji: za rʒɛtʃ]
You are welcome.	**Není zač.** [nɛni: zatʃ]
Any time.	**Je mi potěšením.** [jɛ mɪ poteʃɛni:m]
My pleasure.	**S radostí.** [s radosti:]
Forget it.	**To nestojí za řeč.** [to nɛstoji: za rʒɛtʃ]
Don't worry about it.	**Tím se netrapte.** [ti:m sɛ nɛtraptɛ]

Congratulations. Best wishes

Congratulations!	**Blahopřeju!**
	[blahoprʒɛju!]
Happy birthday!	**Všechno nejlepší k narozeninám!**
	[vʃɛxno nɛjlɛpʃi: k narozɛnɪna:m!]
Merry Christmas!	**Veselé Vánoce!**
	[vɛsɛlɛ: va:notsɛ!]
Happy New Year!	**Šťastný nový rok!**
	[ʃtʲastni: novi: rok!]

Happy Easter!	**Veselé Velikonoce!**
	[vɛsɛlɛ: vɛlɪkonotsɛ!]
Happy Hanukkah!	**Šťastnou Chanuku!**
	[ʃtʲastnou xanuku!]

I'd like to propose a toast.	**Chtěl /Chtěla/ bych pronést přípitek.**
	[xtɛl /xtela/ bɪx pronɛ:st prʒi:pɪtɛk]
Cheers!	**Na zdraví!**
	[na zdravi:!]
Let's drink to …!	**Pojďme se napít na …!**
	[pojdʲmɛ sɛ napi:t na …!]
To our success!	**Na náš úspěch!**
	[na na:ʃ u:spɛx!]
To your success!	**Na váš úspěch!**
	[na va:ʃ u:spɛx!]

Good luck!	**Hodně štěstí!**
	[hodne ʃtesti:!]
Have a nice day!	**Hezký den!**
	[hɛski: dɛn!]
Have a good holiday!	**Hezkou dovolenou!**
	[hɛskou dovolɛnou!]
Have a safe journey!	**Šťastnou cestu!**
	[ʃtʲastnou tsɛstu!]
I hope you get better soon!	**Doufám, že se brzy uzdravíte!**
	[doufa:m, ʒe sɛ brzɪ uzdravi:tɛ!]

Socializing

Why are you sad?

Proč jste smutný /smutná/?
[protʃ jstɛ smutni: /smutna:/?]

Smile! Cheer up!

Usmějte se! Hlavu vzhůru!
[usmnejtɛ sɛ! hlavu vzhu:ru!]

Are you free tonight?

Máte dnes večer čas?
[ma:tɛ dnɛs vɛtʃɛr tʃas?]

May I offer you a drink?

Můžu vám nabídnout něco k pití?
[mu:ʒu va:m nabi:dnout netso k pɪti:?]

Would you like to dance?

Smím prosit?
[smi:m prosi:t?]

Let's go to the movies.

Nechcete jít do kina?
[nɛxtsɛtɛ ji:t do kɪna?]

May I invite you to ...?

Můžu vás pozvat ...?
[mu:ʒu va:s pozvat ...?]

a restaurant

do restaurace
[do rɛstauratsɛ]

the movies

do kina
[do kɪna]

the theater

do divadla
[do dɪvadla]

go for a walk

na procházku
[na proxa:sku]

At what time?

V kolik hodin?
[v kolɪk hodɪn?]

tonight

dnes večer
[dnɛs vɛtʃɛr]

at six

v šest
[v ʃɛst]

at seven

v sedm
[v sɛdm]

at eight

v osm
[v osm]

at nine

v devět
[v dɛvet]

Do you like it here?

Líbí se vám tady?
[li:bi: sɛ va:m tadɪ?]

Are you here with someone?

Jste tady s někým?
[jstɛ tadɪ s neki:m?]

I'm with my friend.

Jsem tady s přítelem /přítelkyní/.
[jsɛm tadɪ s prʒi:tɛlɛm /prʒi:tɛlkɪni:/]

I'm with my friends.	**Jsem tady s přáteli.** [jsɛm tadɪ s prʒaːtɛlɪ]
No, I'm alone.	**Ne, jsem tady sám /sama/.** [nɛ, jsɛm tadɪ saːm /sama/]
Do you have a boyfriend?	**Máš přítele?** [maːʃ prʃiːtɛlɛ?]
I have a boyfriend.	**Mám přítele.** [maːm prʃiːtɛlɛ]
Do you have a girlfriend?	**Máš přítelkyni?** [maːʃ prʃiːtɛlkɪnɪ?]
I have a girlfriend.	**Mám přítelkyni.** [maːm prʃiːtɛlkɪnɪ]
Can I see you again?	**Můžu tě zase vidět?** [muːʒu te zasɛ vɪdet?]
Can I call you?	**Můžu ti zavolat?** [muːʒu tɪ zavolat?]
Call me. (Give me a call.)	**Zavolej mi.** [zavolɛj mɪ]
What's your number?	**Jaké je tvoje číslo?** [jakɛː jɛ tvojɛ tʃiːslo?]
I miss you.	**Stýská se mi po tobě.** [stiːskaː sɛ mɪ po tobe]
You have a beautiful name.	**Máte krásné jméno.** [maːtɛ kraːsnɛː jmɛːno]
I love you.	**Miluju tě.** [mɪluju te]
Will you marry me?	**Vezmeš si mě?** [vɛzmɛʃ sɪ mne?]
You're kidding!	**Děláte si legraci!** [delaːtɛ sɪ lɛgratsɪ!]
I'm just kidding.	**Žertoval /Žertovala/ jsem.** [ʒertoval /ʒertovala/ jsɛm]
Are you serious?	**Myslíte to vážně?** [mɪsliːtɛ to vaːʒne?]
I'm serious.	**Myslím to vážně.** [mɪsliːm to vaːʒne]
Really?!	**Opravdu?!** [opravdu?!]
It's unbelievable!	**To je neuvěřitelné!** [to jɛ nɛuverʒɪtɛlnɛː!]
I don't believe you.	**Nevěřím vám.** [nɛverʒiːm vaːm]
I can't.	**Nemůžu.** [nɛmuːʒu]
I don't know.	**Nevím.** [nɛviːm]
I don't understand you.	**Nerozumím vám.** [nɛrozumiːm vaːm]

Please go away.

Leave me alone!

Odejděte prosím.
[odɛjdetɛ prosi:m]

Nechte mě na pokoji!
[nɛxtɛ mne na pokojɪ!]

I can't stand him.

You are disgusting!

I'll call the police!

Nesnáším ho.
[nɛsna:ʃi:m ho]

Jste odporný!
[jstɛ otporni:!]

Zavolám policii!
[zavola:m polɪtsɪjɪ!]

Sharing impressions. Emotions

I like it.	**Líbí se mi to.** [li:bi: sɛ mɪ to]
Very nice.	**Moc pěkné.** [mots peknɛ:]
That's great!	**To je skvělé!** [to jɛ skvelɛ:!]
It's not bad.	**To není špatné.** [to nɛni: ʃpatnɛ:]

I don't like it.	**Nelíbí se mi to.** [nɛli:bi: sɛ mɪ to]
It's not good.	**To není dobře.** [to nɛni: dobrʒɛ]
It's bad.	**To je špatné.** [to jɛ ʃpatnɛ:]
It's very bad.	**Je to moc špatné.** [jɛ to mots ʃpatnɛ:]
It's disgusting.	**To je odporné.** [to jɛ otpornɛ:]

I'm happy.	**Jsem šťastný /šťastná/.** [jsɛm ʃťastni: /ʃťastna:/]
I'm content.	**Jsem spokojený /spokojená/.** [jsɛm spokojɛni: /spokojɛna:/]
I'm in love.	**Jsem zamilovaný /zamilovaná/.** [jsɛm zamɪlovani: /zamɪlovana:/]
I'm calm.	**Jsem klidný /klidná/.** [jsɛm klɪdni: /klɪdna:/]
I'm bored.	**Nudím se.** [nudi:m sɛ]

I'm tired.	**Jsem unavený /unavená/.** [jsɛm unavɛni: /unavɛna:/]
I'm sad.	**Jsem smutný /smutná/.** [jsɛm smutni: /smutna:/]
I'm frightened.	**Jsem vystrašený /vystrašená/.** [jsɛm vɪstraʃɛni: /vɪstraʃɛna:/]

I'm angry.	**Zlobím se.** [zlobi:m sɛ]
I'm worried.	**Mám starosti.** [ma:m starostɪ]
I'm nervous.	**Jsem nervózní.** [jsɛm nɛrvózni:]

I'm jealous. (envious)

I'm surprised.

I'm perplexed.

Žárlím.
[ʒaːrliːm]

Jsem překvapený /překvapená/.
[jsɛm prʒɛkvapɛniː /prʒɛkvapɛnaː/]

Jsem zmatený /zmatená/.
[jsɛm zmatɛniː /zmatɛnaː/]

Problems. Accidents

I've got a problem. | **Mám problém.** [ma:m problɛ:m]

We've got a problem. | **Máme problém.** [ma:mɛ problɛ:m]

I'm lost. | **Ztratil /Ztratila/ jsem se.** [stratɪl /stratɪla/ jsɛm sɛ]

I missed the last bus (train). | **Zmeškal /Zmeškala/ jsem poslední autobus (vlak).** [zmɛʃkal /zmɛʃkala/ jsɛm poslɛdni: autobus (vlak)]

I don't have any money left. | **Už nemám žádné peníze.** [uʒ nɛma:m ʒa:dnɛ: pɛni:zɛ]

I've lost my ... | **Ztratil /Ztratila/ jsem ...** [stratɪl /stratɪla/ jsɛm ...]

Someone stole my ... | **Někdo mi ukradl ...** [nɛgdo mɪ ukradl ...]

passport | **pas** [pas]

wallet | **peněženku** [pɛnɛʒɛŋku]

papers | **dokumenty** [dokumɛntɪ]

ticket | **vstupenku** [vstupɛŋku]

money | **peníze** [pɛni:zɛ]

handbag | **kabelku** [kabɛlku]

camera | **fotoaparát** [fotoapara:t]

laptop | **počítač** [potʃi:tatʃ]

tablet computer | **tablet** [tablɛt]

mobile phone | **mobilní telefon** [mobɪlni: tɛlɛfon]

Help me! | **Pomozte mi!** [pomoztɛ mɪ!]

What's happened? | **Co se stalo?** [tso sɛ stalo?]

fire	**požár** [poʒaːr]
shooting	**střelba** [strʒɛlba]
murder	**vražda** [vraʒda]
explosion	**výbuch** [viːbux]
fight	**rvačka** [rvatʃka]

Call the police!	**Zavolejte policii!** [zavolɛjtɛ polɪtsɪjɪ!]
Please hurry up!	**Pospěšte si prosím!** [pospeʃtɛ sɪ prosiːm!]
I'm looking for the police station.	**Hledám policejní stanici.** [hlɛdaːm polɪtsɛjni: stanɪtsɪ]
I need to make a call.	**Potřebuju si zavolat.** [potrʒɛbuju sɪ zavolat]
May I use your phone?	**Můžu si od vás zavolat?** [muːʒu sɪ od vaːs zavolat?]

I've been ...	**Byl /Byla/ jsem ...** [bɪl /bɪla/ jsɛm ...]
mugged	**přepaden /přepadena/** [prʃɛpadɛn /prʃɛpadɛna/]
robbed	**oloupen /oloupena/** [oloupɛn /oloupɛna/]
raped	**znásilněna** [znaːsɪlnena]
attacked (beaten up)	**napaden /napadena/** [napadɛn /napadɛna/]

Are you all right?	**Jste v pořádku?** [jstɛ v porʒaːtku?]
Did you see who it was?	**Viděl /Viděla/ jste, kdo to byl?** [vɪdel /vɪdela/ jstɛ, gdo to bɪl?]
Would you be able to recognize the person?	**Poznal /Poznala/ byste toho člověka?** [poznal /poznala/ bɪstɛ toho tʃloveka?]
Are you sure?	**Jste si tím jist /jista/?** [jstɛ sɪ tiːm jɪst /jɪsta/?]

Please calm down.	**Uklidněte se, prosím.** [uklɪdnetɛ sɛ, prosiːm]
Take it easy!	**Uklidněte se!** [uklɪdnetɛ sɛ!]
Don't worry!	**Nebojte se!** [nɛbojtɛ sɛ!]
Everything will be fine.	**Všechno bude v pořádku.** [vʃɛxno budɛ v porʒaːtku]
Everything's all right.	**Vše v pořádku.** [vʃɛ v porʒaːtku]

Come here, please.

I have some questions for you.

Wait a moment, please.

Do you have any I.D.?

Thanks. You can leave now.

Hands behind your head!

You're under arrest!

Pojďte sem, prosím.
[pojdʲtɛ sɛm, prosiːm]

Mám na vás několik otázek.
[maːm na vaːs nekolɪk otaːzɛk]

Okamžik, prosím.
[okamʒɪk, prosiːm]

Máte nějaký průkaz totožnosti?
[maːtɛ nejakiː pruːkaz totoʒnostɪ?]

Díky. Teď můžete odejít.
[diːkɪ. tɛdʲ muːʒetɛ odɛjiːt]

Ruce za hlavu!
[rutsɛ za hlavu!]

Jste zatčen /zatčena/!
[jstɛ zattʃɛn /zattʃɛna/!]

Health problems

Please help me.	**Prosím vás, pomozte mi.** [prosi:m va:s, pomoztɛ mɪ]
I don't feel well.	**Necítím se dobře.** [nɛtsi:ti:m sɛ dobrʒɛ]
My husband doesn't feel well.	**Můj manžel se necítí dobře.** [mu:j manʒel sɛ nɛtsi:ti: dobrʒe]
My son ...	**Můj syn ...** [mu:j sɪn ...]
My father ...	**Můj otec ...** [mu:j otɛts ...]
My wife doesn't feel well.	**Moje manželka se necítí dobře.** [mojɛ manʒelka sɛ nɛtsi:ti: dobrʒe]
My daughter ...	**Moje dcera ...** [mojɛ dtsɛra ...]
My mother ...	**Moje matka ...** [mojɛ matka ...]
I've got a ...	**Bolí mě ...** [boli: mne ...]
headache	**hlava** [hlava]
sore throat	**v krku** [v krku]
stomach ache	**žaludek** [ʒaludɛk]
toothache	**zub** [zup]
I feel dizzy.	**Mám závratě.** [ma:m za:vrate]
He has a fever.	**On má horečku.** [on ma: horɛtʃku]
She has a fever.	**Ona má horečku.** [ona ma: horɛtʃku]
I can't breathe.	**Nemůžu dýchat.** [nɛmu:ʒu di:xat]
I'm short of breath.	**Nemůžu se nadechnout.** [nɛmu:ʒu sɛ nadɛxnout]
I am asthmatic.	**Jsem astmatik /astmatička/.** [jsɛm astmatɪk /astmatɪtʃka/]
I am diabetic.	**Jsem diabetik /diabetička/.** [jsɛm dɪabɛtɪk /dɪabɛtɪtʃka/]

I can't sleep.	**Nemůžu spát.** [nɛmuːʒu spaːt]
food poisoning	**otrava z jídla** [otrava z jiːdla]

It hurts here.	**Tady to bolí.** [tadɪ to boliː]
Help me!	**Pomozte mi!** [pomoztɛ mɪ!]
I am here!	**Tady jsem!** [tadɪ jsɛm!]
We are here!	**Tady jsme!** [tadɪ jsmɛ!]
Get me out of here!	**Dostaňte mě odtud!** [dostaɲtɛ mne odtut!]
I need a doctor.	**Potřebuju doktora.** [potrʒɛbuju doktora]
I can't move.	**Nemůžu se hýbat.** [nɛmuːʒu sɛ hiːbat]
I can't move my legs.	**Nemůžu hýbat nohama.** [nɛmuːʒu hiːbat nohama]

I have a wound.	**Jsem zraněný /zraněná/.** [jsɛm zraneniː /zranenaː/]
Is it serious?	**Je to vážné?** [jɛ to vaːʒnɛ:?]
My documents are in my pocket.	**Doklady mám v kapse.** [dokladɪ maːm v kapsɛ]
Calm down!	**Uklidněte se!** [uklɪdnetɛ sɛ!]
May I use your phone?	**Můžu si od vás zavolat?** [muːʒu sɪ od vaːs zavolat?]

Call an ambulance!	**Zavolejte sanitku!** [zavolɛjtɛ sanɪtku!]
It's urgent!	**Je to urgentní!** [jɛ to urgɛntniː!]
It's an emergency!	**To je pohotovost!** [to jɛ pohotovost!]
Please hurry up!	**Prosím vás, pospěšte si!** [prosiːm vaːs, pospeʃtɛ sɪ!]
Would you please call a doctor?	**Zavolal /Zavolala/ byste prosím lékaře?** [zavolal /zavolala/ bɪstɛ prosiːm lɛːkarʒɛ?]
Where is the hospital?	**Kde je nemocnice?** [gdɛ jɛ nɛmotsnɪtsɛ?]

How are you feeling?	**Jak se cítíte?** [jak sɛ tsiːtiːtɛ?]
Are you all right?	**Jste v pořádku?** [jstɛ v porʒaːtku?]

What's happened?

Co se stalo?
[tso sɛ stalo?]

I feel better now.

Teď už se cítím líp.
[tɛdʲ uʒ sɛ tsiːtiːm liːp]

It's OK.

To je v pořádku.
[to jɛ v porʒaːtku]

It's all right.

To je v pořádku.
[to jɛ v porʒaːtku]

At the pharmacy

pharmacy (drugstore)	**lékárna** [lɛːkaːrna]
24-hour pharmacy	**non-stop lékárna** [non-stop lɛːkaːrna]
Where is the closest pharmacy?	**Kde je nejbližší lékárna?** [gdɛ jɛ nɛjblɪʒʃiː lɛːkaːrna?]
Is it open now?	**Mají teď otevřeno?** [majiː tɛdʲ otɛvrʒɛno?]
At what time does it open?	**V kolik hodin otvírají?** [v kolɪk hodɪn otviːrajiː?]
At what time does it close?	**V kolik hodin zavírají?** [v kolɪk hodɪn zaviːrajiː?]
Is it far?	**Je to daleko?** [jɛ to dalɛko?]
Can I get there on foot?	**Dostanu se tam pěšky?** [dostanu sɛ tam pɛʃkɪ?]
Can you show me on the map?	**Můžete mi to ukázat na mapě?** [muːʒetɛ mɪ to ukaːzat na mapɛ?]
Please give me something for ...	**Můžete mi prosím vás dát něco na ...** [muːʒetɛ mɪ prosiːm vaːs daːt netso na]
a headache	**bolení hlavy** [bolɛniː hlavɪ]
a cough	**kašel** [kaʃɛl]
a cold	**nachlazení** [naxlazɛniː]
the flu	**chřipka** [xrʃɪpka]
a fever	**horečka** [horɛtʃka]
a stomach ache	**bolesti v žaludku** [bolɛstɪ v ʒalutku]
nausea	**nucení na zvracení** [nutsɛniː na zvratsɛniː]
diarrhea	**průjem** [pruːjɛm]
constipation	**zácpa** [zaːtspa]

pain in the back	**bolest v zádech** [bolɛst v zaːdɛx]
chest pain	**bolest na hrudi** [bolɛst na hrudɪ]
side stitch	**boční steh** [botʃniː stɛh]
abdominal pain	**bolest břicha** [bolɛst brʒɪxa]

pill	**pilulka** [pɪlulka]
ointment, cream	**mast, krém** [mast, krɛːm]
syrup	**sirup** [sɪrup]
spray	**sprej** [sprɛj]
drops	**kapky** [kapkɪ]

You need to go to the hospital.	**Musíte jít do nemocnice.** [musiːtɛ jiːt do nɛmotsnɪtsɛ]
health insurance	**zdravotní pojištění** [zdravotniː pojɪʃteniː]
prescription	**předpis** [prʃɛtpɪs]
insect repellant	**repelent proti hmyzu** [rɛpɛlɛnt protɪ hmɪzu]
Band Aid	**náplast** [naːplast]

The bare minimum

Excuse me, ...	**Promiňte, ...** [prɔmɪnˈtɛ, ...]
Hello.	**Dobrý den.** [dɔbriː dɛn]
Thank you.	**Děkuji.** [dɛkujɪ]
Good bye.	**Na shledanou.** [na sxlɛdanou]
Yes.	**Ano.** [anɔ]
No.	**Ne.** [nɛ]
I don't know.	**Nevím.** [nɛviːm]
Where?	Where to?	When?	**Kde?	Kam?	Kdy?** [gdɛ?	kam?	gdɪ?]
I need ...	**Potřebuju ...** [pɔtrʒɛbuju ...]
I want ...	**Chci ...** [xtsɪ ...]
Do you have ...?	**Máte ...?** [maːtɛ ...?]
Is there a ... here?	**Je tady ...?** [jɛ tadɪ ...?]
May I ...?	**Můžu ...?** [muːʒu ...?]
..., please (polite request)	**..., prosím** [..., prosiːm]
I'm looking for ...	**Hledám ...** [hlɛdaːm ...]
the restroom	**toaletu** [tɔalɛtu]
an ATM	**bankomat** [baŋkɔmat]
a pharmacy (drugstore)	**lékárnu** [lɛːkaːrnu]
a hospital	**nemocnici** [nɛmɔtsnɪtsɪ]
the police station	**policejní stanici** [pɔlɪtsɛjniː stanɪtsɪ]
the subway	**metro** [mɛtrɔ]

a taxi	**taxík** [taksi:k]
the train station	**vlakové nádraží** [vlakovɛ: naːdraʒiː]

My name is …	**Jmenuju se …** [jmɛnuju sɛ …]
What's your name?	**Jak se jmenujete?** [jak sɛ jmɛnujɛtɛ?]
Could you please help me?	**Můžete mi prosím pomoct?** [muːʒetɛ mɪ prosiːm pomotst?]
I've got a problem.	**Mám problém.** [maːm problɛːm]
I don't feel well.	**Necítím se dobře.** [nɛtsiːtiːm sɛ dobrʒɛ]
Call an ambulance!	**Zavolejte sanitku!** [zavolɛjtɛ sanɪtku!]
May I make a call?	**Můžu si zavolat?** [muːʒu sɪ zavolat?]

I'm sorry.	**Omlouvám se.** [omlouvaːm sɛ]
You're welcome.	**Není zač.** [nɛniː zatʃ]

I, me	**Já** [jaː]
you (inform.)	**ty** [tɪ]
he	**on** [on]
she	**ona** [ona]
they (masc.)	**oni** [onɪ]
they (fem.)	**ony** [onɪ]
we	**my** [mɪ]
you (pl)	**vy** [vɪ]
you (sg, form.)	**vy** [vɪ]

ENTRANCE	**VCHOD** [vxot]
EXIT	**VÝCHOD** [viːxot]
OUT OF ORDER	**MIMO PROVOZ** [mɪmo provos]
CLOSED	**ZAVŘENO** [zavrʒɛno]

OPEN	**OTEVŘENO** [otɛvrʒɛno]
FOR WOMEN	**ŽENY** [ʒenɪ]
FOR MEN	**MUŽI** [muʒɪ]

CONCISE
DICTIONARY

This section contains more
than 1,500 useful words
arranged alphabetically.
The dictionary includes a lot
of gastronomic terms and
will be helpful when ordering
food at a restaurant or buying
groceries

T&P Books Publishing

DICTIONARY CONTENTS

1. Time. Calendar	74
2. Numbers. Numerals	75
3. Humans. Family	76
4. Human body	77
5. Medicine. Diseases. Drugs	79
6. Feelings. Emotions. Conversation	80
7. Clothing. Personal accessories	81
8. City. Urban institutions	82
9. Money. Finances	84
10. Transportation	85
11. Food. Part 1	86
12. Food. Part 2	87
13. House. Apartment. Part 1	89
14. House. Apartment. Part 2	90
15. Professions. Social status	91
16. Sport	92

T&P Books Publishing

17. Foreign languages. Orthography	94
18. The Earth. Geography	95
19. Countries of the world. Part 1	96
20. Countries of the world. Part 2	97
21. Weather. Natural disasters	99
22. Animals. Part 1	100
23. Animals. Part 2	101
24. Trees. Plants	102
25. Various useful words	103
26. Modifiers. Adjectives. Part 1	105
27. Modifiers. Adjectives. Part 2	106
28. Verbs. Part 1	107
29. Verbs. Part 2	108
30. Verbs. Part 3	110

T&P Books Publishing

time	čas (m)	[tʃas]
hour	hodina (ž)	[hodɪna]
half an hour	půlhodina (ž)	[puːlhodɪna]
minute	minuta (ž)	[mɪnuta]
second	sekunda (ž)	[sɛkunda]
today (adv)	dnes	[dnɛs]
tomorrow (adv)	zítra	[ziːtra]
yesterday (adv)	včera	[vtʃɛra]
Monday	pondělí (s)	[pondeliː]
Tuesday	úterý (s)	[uːtɛriː]
Wednesday	středa (ž)	[strʃɛda]
Thursday	čtvrtek (m)	[tʃtvrtɛk]
Friday	pátek (m)	[paːtɛk]
Saturday	sobota (ž)	[sobota]
Sunday	neděle (ž)	[nɛdelɛ]
day	den (m)	[dɛn]
working day	pracovní den (m)	[pratsovniː dɛn]
public holiday	sváteční den (m)	[svaːtɛtʃni dɛn]
weekend	víkend (m)	[viːkɛnt]
week	týden (m)	[tiːdɛn]
last week (adv)	minulý týden	[mɪnuli tiːdɛn]
next week (adv)	příští týden	[prʃiːʃti tiːdɛn]
sunrise	východ (m) slunce	[viːxod sluntsɛ]
sunset	západ (m) slunce	[zaːpat sluntsɛ]
in the morning	ráno	[raːno]
in the afternoon	odpoledne	[otpolɛdnɛ]
in the evening	večer	[vɛtʃɛr]
tonight (this evening)	dnes večer	[dnɛs vɛtʃɛr]
at night	v noci	[v notsɪ]
midnight	půlnoc (ž)	[puːlnots]
January	leden (m)	[lɛdɛn]
February	únor (m)	[uːnor]
March	březen (m)	[brʒɛzɛn]
April	duben (m)	[dubɛn]
May	květen (m)	[kvetɛn]
June	červen (m)	[tʃɛrvɛn]

July	červenec (m)	[tʃɛrvɛnɛts]
August	srpen (m)	[srpɛn]
September	září (s)	[zaːrʒiː]
October	říjen (m)	[rʒiːjɛn]
November	listopad (m)	[lɪstopat]
December	prosinec (m)	[prosɪnɛts]

in spring	na jaře	[na jarʒɛ]
in summer	v létě	[v lɛːte]
in fall	na podzim	[na podzɪm]
in winter	v zimě	[v zɪmne]

month	měsíc (m)	[mnesiːts]
season (summer, etc.)	období (s)	[obdobiː]
year	rok (m)	[rok]
century	století (s)	[stolɛtiː]

2. Numbers. Numerals

digit, figure	číslice (ž)	[tʃiːslɪtsɛ]
number	číslo (s)	[tʃiːslo]
minus sign	minus (m)	[miːnus]
plus sign	plus (m)	[plus]
sum, total	součet (m)	[soutʃɛt]

first (adj)	první	[prvniː]
second (adj)	druhý	[druhiː]
third (adj)	třetí	[trʃɛtiː]

0 zero	nula (ž)	[nula]
1 one	jeden	[jɛdɛn]
2 two	dva	[dva]
3 three	tři	[trʃɪ]
4 four	čtyři	[tʃtɪrʒɪ]

5 five	pět	[pet]
6 six	šest	[ʃɛst]
7 seven	sedm	[sɛdm]
8 eight	osm	[osm]
9 nine	devět	[dɛvet]
10 ten	deset	[dɛsɛt]

11 eleven	jedenáct	[jɛdɛnaːtst]
12 twelve	dvanáct	[dvanaːtst]
13 thirteen	třináct	[trʃinaːtst]
14 fourteen	čtrnáct	[tʃtrnaːtst]
15 fifteen	patnáct	[patnaːtst]

16 sixteen	šestnáct	[ʃɛstnaːtst]
17 seventeen	sedmnáct	[sɛdmnaːtst]

18 eighteen	osmnáct	[osmnaːʦt]
19 nineteen	devatenáct	[dɛvatɛnaːʦt]
20 twenty	dvacet	[dvaʦɛt]
30 thirty	třicet	[trʃɪʦɛt]
40 forty	čtyřicet	[ʧtɪrʒɪʦɛt]
50 fifty	padesát	[padesaːt]
60 sixty	šedesát	[ʃɛdɛsaːt]
70 seventy	sedmdesát	[sɛdmdɛsaːt]
80 eighty	osmdesát	[osmdɛsaːt]
90 ninety	devadesát	[dɛvadɛsaːt]
100 one hundred	sto	[sto]
200 two hundred	dvě stě	[dve ste]
300 three hundred	tři sta	[trʃɪ sta]
400 four hundred	čtyři sta	[ʧtɪrʒɪ sta]
500 five hundred	pět set	[pet sɛt]
600 six hundred	šest set	[ʃɛst sɛt]
700 seven hundred	sedm set	[sɛdm sɛt]
800 eight hundred	osm set	[osm sɛt]
900 nine hundred	devět set	[dɛvet sɛt]
1000 one thousand	tisíc (m)	[tɪsiːʦ]
10000 ten thousand	deset tisíc	[dɛsɛt tɪsiːʦ]
one hundred thousand	sto tisíc	[sto tɪsiːʦ]
million	milión (m)	[mɪlɪoːn]
billion	miliarda (ž)	[mɪlɪarda]

3. Humans. Family

man (adult male)	muž (m)	[muʃ]
young man	jinoch (m)	[jɪnox]
teenager	výrostek (m)	[viːrostɛk]
woman	žena (ž)	[ʒena]
girl (young woman)	slečna (ž)	[slɛʧna]
age	věk (m)	[vek]
adult (adj)	dospělý	[dospeliː]
middle-aged (adj)	středního věku	[strʃɛdniːho veku]
elderly (adj)	starší	[starʃiː]
old (adj)	starý	[stariː]
old man	stařec (m)	[starʒɛʦ]
old woman	stařena (ž)	[starʒɛna]
retirement	důchod (m)	[duːxot]
to retire (from job)	odejít do důchodu	[odɛjiːt do duːxodu]
retiree	důchodce (m)	[duːxodʦɛ]

mother	matka (ž)	[matka]
father	otec (m)	[otɛʦ]
son	syn (m)	[sɪn]
daughter	dcera (ž)	[dʦɛra]
brother	bratr (m)	[bratr]
elder brother	starší bratr (m)	[starʃi: bratr]
younger brother	mladší bratr (m)	[mladʃi: bratr]
sister	sestra (ž)	[sɛstra]
elder sister	starší sestra (ž)	[starʃi: sɛstra]
younger sister	mladší sestra (ž)	[mladʃi: sɛstra]
parents	rodiče (m mn)	[rodɪʧɛ]
child	dítě (s)	[di:tɛ]
children	děti (ž mn)	[detɪ]
stepmother	nevlastní matka (ž)	[nɛvlastni: matka]
stepfather	nevlastní otec (m)	[nɛvlastni: otɛʦ]
grandmother	babička (ž)	[babɪʧka]
grandfather	dědeček (m)	[dedɛʧɛk]
grandson	vnuk (m)	[vnuk]
granddaughter	vnučka (ž)	[vnuʧka]
grandchildren	vnuci (m mn)	[vnuʦɪ]
uncle	strýc (m)	[stri:ʦ]
aunt	teta (ž)	[tɛta]
nephew	synovec (m)	[sɪnovɛʦ]
niece	neteř (ž)	[nɛtɛrʃ]
wife	žena (ž)	[ʒena]
husband	muž (m)	[muʃ]
married (masc.)	ženatý	[ʒenati:]
married (fem.)	vdaná	[vdana:]
widow	vdova (ž)	[vdova]
widower	vdovec (m)	[vdovɛʦ]
name (first name)	jméno (s)	[jmɛ:no]
surname (last name)	příjmení (s)	[prʃi:jmɛni:]
relative	příbuzný (m)	[prʃi:buzni:]
friend (masc.)	přítel (m)	[prʃi:tɛl]
friendship	přátelství (s)	[prʃa:tɛlstvi:]
partner	partner (m)	[partnɛr]
superior (n)	vedoucí (m)	[vɛdouʦi:]
colleague	kolega (m)	[kolɛga]
neighbors	sousedé (m mn)	[sousɛdɛ:]

4. Human body

| organism (body) | organismus (m) | [organɪzmus] |
| body | tělo (s) | [telo] |

heart	**srdce** (s)	[srdtsɛ]
blood	**krev** (ž)	[krɛf]
brain	**mozek** (m)	[mozɛk]
nerve	**nerv** (m)	[nɛrf]
bone	**kost** (ž)	[kost]
skeleton	**kostra** (ž)	[kostra]
spine (backbone)	**páteř** (ž)	[paːtɛrʃ]
rib	**žebro** (s)	[ʒebro]
skull	**lebka** (ž)	[lɛpka]
muscle	**sval** (m)	[sval]
lungs	**plíce** (ž mn)	[pliːtsɛ]
skin	**pleť** (ž)	[plɛtʲ]
head	**hlava** (ž)	[hlava]
face	**obličej** (ž)	[oblɪtʃɛj]
nose	**nos** (m)	[nos]
forehead	**čelo** (s)	[tʃɛlo]
cheek	**tvář** (ž)	[tvaːrʃ]
mouth	**ústa** (s mn)	[uːsta]
tongue	**jazyk** (m)	[jazɪk]
tooth	**zub** (m)	[zup]
lips	**rty** (m mn)	[rtɪ]
chin	**brada** (ž)	[brada]
ear	**ucho** (s)	[uxo]
neck	**krk** (m)	[krk]
throat	**hrdlo** (s)	[hrdlo]
eye	**oko** (s)	[oko]
pupil	**zornice** (ž)	[zornɪtsɛ]
eyebrow	**obočí** (s)	[obotʃiː]
eyelash	**řasa** (ž)	[rʒasa]
hair	**vlasy** (m mn)	[vlasɪ]
hairstyle	**účes** (m)	[uːtʃɛs]
mustache	**vousy** (m mn)	[vousɪ]
beard	**plnovous** (m)	[plnovous]
to have (a beard, etc.)	**nosit**	[nosɪt]
bald (adj)	**lysý**	[lɪsiː]
hand	**ruka** (ž)	[ruka]
arm	**ruka** (ž)	[ruka]
finger	**prst** (m)	[prst]
nail	**nehet** (m)	[nɛhɛt]
palm	**dlaň** (ž)	[dlanʲ]
shoulder	**rameno** (s)	[ramɛno]
leg	**noha** (ž)	[noha]
foot	**chodidlo** (s)	[xodɪdlo]

| knee | koleno (s) | [kolɛno] |
| heel | pata (ž) | [pata] |

back	záda (s mn)	[za:da]
waist	pás (m)	[pa:s]
beauty mark	mateřské znaménko (s)	[matɛrʃkɛ: znamɛ:ŋko]

5. Medicine. Diseases. Drugs

health	zdraví (s)	[zdravi:]
well (not sick)	zdravý	[zdravi:]
sickness	nemoc (ž)	[nɛmoʦ]
to be sick	být nemocný	[bi:t nɛmoʦni:]
ill, sick (adj)	nemocný	[nɛmoʦni:]

cold (illness)	nachlazení (s)	[naxlazɛni:]
to catch a cold	nachladit se	[naxladɪt sɛ]
tonsillitis	angína (ž)	[angi:na]
pneumonia	zápal (m) plic	[za:pal plɪʦ]
flu, influenza	chřipka (ž)	[xrʃɪpka]

runny nose (coryza)	rýma (ž)	[ri:ma]
cough	kašel (m)	[kaʃɛl]
to cough (vi)	kašlat	[kaʃlat]
to sneeze (vi)	kýchat	[ki:xat]

stroke	mozková mrtvice (ž)	[moskova: mrtvɪʦɛ]
heart attack	infarkt (m)	[ɪnfarkt]
allergy	alergie (ž)	[alɛrgɪɛ]
asthma	astma (s)	[astma]
diabetes	cukrovka (ž)	[ʦukrofka]

tumor	nádor (m)	[na:dor]
cancer	rakovina (ž)	[rakovɪna]
alcoholism	alkoholismus (m)	[alkoholɪzmus]
AIDS	AIDS (m)	[ajts]
fever	zimnice (ž)	[zɪmnɪʦɛ]
seasickness	mořská nemoc (ž)	[morʃska: nɛmoʦ]

bruise (hématome)	modřina (ž)	[modrʒɪna]
bump (lump)	boule (ž)	[boulɛ]
to limp (vi)	kulhat	[kulhat]
dislocation	vykloubení (s)	[vɪkloubɛni:]
to dislocate (vt)	vykloubit	[vɪkloubɪt]

fracture	zlomenina (ž)	[zlomɛnɪna]
burn (injury)	popálenina (ž)	[popa:lɛnɪna]
injury	pohmoždění (s)	[pohmoʒdeni:]
pain, ache	bolest (ž)	[bolɛst]
toothache	bolení (s) zubů	[bolɛni: zubu:]

to sweat (perspire)	potit se	[potɪt sɛ]
deaf (adj)	hluchý	[hluxi:]
mute (adj)	němý	[nemi:]

immunity	imunita (ž)	[ɪmunɪta]
virus	virus (m)	[vɪrus]
microbe	mikrob (m)	[mɪkrop]
bacterium	baktérie (ž)	[baktɛ:rɪe]
infection	infekce (ž)	[ɪnfɛktsɛ]

hospital	nemocnice (ž)	[nɛmotsnɪtsɛ]
cure	léčení (s)	[lɛ:tʃɛni:]
to vaccinate (vt)	dělat očkování	[delat otʃkova:ni:]
to be in a coma	být v kómatu	[bi:t v ko:matu]
intensive care	reanimace (ž)	[rɛanɪmatsɛ]
symptom	příznak (m)	[prʃi:znak]
pulse (heartbeat)	tep (m)	[tɛp]

6. Feelings. Emotions. Conversation

I, me	já	[ja:]
you	ty	[tɪ]
he	on	[on]
she	ona	[ona]

we	my	[mɪ]
you (to a group)	vy	[vɪ]
they (inanim.)	ony	[onɪ]
they (anim.)	oni	[onɪ]

Hello! (fam.)	Dobrý den!	[dobri: dɛn]
Hello! (form.)	Dobrý den!	[dobri: dɛn]
Good morning!	Dobré jitro!	[dobrɛ: jɪtro]
Good afternoon!	Dobrý den!	[dobri: dɛn]
Good evening!	Dobrý večer!	[dobri: vɛtʃɛr]

to say hello	zdravit	[zdravɪt]
to greet (vt)	zdravit	[zdravɪt]
How are you?	Jak se máte?	[jak sɛ ma:tɛ]
Bye-Bye! Goodbye!	Na shledanou!	[na sxlɛdanou]
Thank you!	Děkuji!	[dekujɪ]

feelings	pocity (m mn)	[potsɪtɪ]
to be hungry	mít hlad	[mi:t hlat]
to be thirsty	mít žízeň	[mi:t ʒi:zɛnʲ]
tired (adj)	unavený	[unavɛni:]

to be worried	znepokojovat se	[znɛpokojovat sɛ]
to be nervous	být nervózní	[bi:t nɛrvo:zni:]
hope	naděje (ž)	[nadejɛ]

to hope (vi, vt)	doufat	[doufat]
character	povaha (ž)	[povaha]
modest (adj)	skromný	[skromni:]
lazy (adj)	líný	[li:ni:]
generous (adj)	štědrý	[ʃtedri:]
talented (adj)	nadaný	[nadani:]
honest (adj)	poctivý	[potstɪvi:]
serious (adj)	vážný	[va:ʒni:]
shy, timid (adj)	nesmělý	[nɛsmneli:]
sincere (adj)	upřímný	[uprʃi:mni:]
coward	zbabělec (m)	[zbabelɛts]
to sleep (vi)	spát	[spa:t]
dream	sen (m)	[sɛn]
bed	lůžko (s)	[lu:ʃko]
pillow	polštář (m)	[polʃta:rʃ]
insomnia	nespavost (ž)	[nɛspavost]
to go to bed	jít spát	[ji:t spa:t]
nightmare	noční můra (ž)	[notʃni: mu:ra]
alarm clock	budík (m)	[budi:k]
smile	úsměv (m)	[u:smnef]
to smile (vi)	usmívat se	[usmi:vat sɛ]
to laugh (vi)	smát se	[sma:t sɛ]
quarrel	hádka (ž)	[ha:tka]
insult	urážka (ž)	[ura:ʃka]
resentment	urážka (ž)	[ura:ʃka]
angry (mad)	rozčilený	[roztʃɪleni:]

7. Clothing. Personal accessories

clothes	oblečení (s)	[oblɛtʃɛni:]
coat (overcoat)	kabát (m)	[kaba:t]
fur coat	kožich (m)	[koʒɪx]
jacket (e.g., leather ~)	bunda (ž)	[bunda]
raincoat (trenchcoat, etc.)	plášť (m)	[pla:ʃtʲ]
shirt (button shirt)	košile (ž)	[koʃɪlɛ]
pants	kalhoty (ž mn)	[kalhotɪ]
suit jacket	sako (s)	[sako]
suit	pánský oblek (m)	[pa:nski: oblɛk]
dress (frock)	šaty (m mn)	[ʃatɪ]
skirt	sukně (ž)	[sukne]
T-shirt	tričko (s)	[trɪtʃko]
bathrobe	župan (m)	[ʒupan]
pajamas	pyžamo (s)	[piʒamo]

workwear	pracovní oděv (m)	[pratsovni: odef]
underwear	spodní prádlo (s)	[spodni: pra:dlo]
socks	ponožky (ž mn)	[ponoʃkɪ]
bra	podprsenka (ž)	[potprsɛŋka]
pantyhose	punčochové kalhoty (ž mn)	[puntʃoxovɛ: kalgotɪ]
stockings (thigh highs)	punčochy (ž mn)	[puntʃoxɪ]
bathing suit	plavky (ž mn)	[plafkɪ]

hat	čepice (ž)	[tʃɛprtsɛ]
footwear	obuv (ž)	[obuf]
boots (e.g., cowboy ~)	holínky (ž mn)	[holi:ŋkɪ]
heel	podpatek (m)	[potpatɛk]
shoestring	tkanička (ž)	[tkanɪtʃka]
shoe polish	krém (m) na boty	[krɛ:m na botɪ]

cotton (n)	bavlna (ž)	[bavlna]
wool (n)	vlna (ž)	[vlna]
fur (n)	kožešina (ž)	[koʒɛʃɪna]

gloves	rukavice (ž mn)	[rukavɪtsɛ]
mittens	palčáky (m mn)	[paltʃa:kɪ]
scarf (muffler)	šála (ž)	[ʃa:la]
glasses (eyeglasses)	brýle (ž mn)	[bri:lɛ]
umbrella	deštník (m)	[dɛʃtni:k]

tie (necktie)	kravata (ž)	[kravata]
handkerchief	kapesník (m)	[kapesni:k]
comb	hřeben (m)	[hrʒɛbɛn]
hairbrush	kartáč (m) na vlasy	[karta:tʃ na vlasɪ]

buckle	spona (ž)	[spona]
belt	pás (m)	[pa:s]
purse	kabelka (ž)	[kabɛlka]

collar	límec (m)	[li:mɛts]
pocket	kapsa (ž)	[kapsa]
sleeve	rukáv (m)	[ruka:f]
fly (on trousers)	poklopec (m)	[poklopɛts]

zipper (fastener)	zip (m)	[zɪp]
button	knoflík (m)	[knofli:k]
to get dirty (vi)	ušpinit se	[uʃpɪnɪt sɛ]
stain (mark, spot)	skvrna (ž)	[skvrna]

8. City. Urban institutions

store	obchod (m)	[obxot]
shopping mall	obchodní středisko (s)	[obxodni: strʃɛdɪsko]
supermarket	supermarket (m)	[supɛrmarket]
shoe store	obchod (m) s obuví	[obxot s obuvi:]

bookstore	knihkupectví (s)	[knɪxkupɛtstvi:]
drugstore, pharmacy	lékárna (ž)	[lɛ:ka:rna]
bakery	pekařství (s)	[pɛkarʃstvi:]
pastry shop	cukrárna (ž)	[tsukra:rna]
grocery store	smíšené zboží (s)	[smiʃɛnɛ: zboʒi:]
butcher shop	řeznictví (s)	[rʒɛznɪtstvi:]
produce store	zelinářství (s)	[zɛlɪna:rʃstvi:]
market	tržnice (ž)	[trʒnɪtsɛ]

hair salon	holičství (s)	[holɪtʃstvi:
	a kadeřnictví	a kadɛrʒnɪtstvi:]
post office	pošta (ž)	[poʃta]
dry cleaners	čistírna (ž)	[tʃɪsti:rna]
circus	cirkus (m)	[tsɪrkus]
zoo	zoologická zahrada (ž)	[zoologɪtska: zahrada]

theater	divadlo (s)	[dɪvadlo]
movie theater	biograf (m)	[bɪograf]
museum	muzeum (s)	[muzɛum]
library	knihovna (ž)	[knɪhovna]

mosque	mešita (ž)	[mɛʃɪta]
synagogue	synagóga (ž)	[sinago:ga]
cathedral	katedrála (ž)	[katɛdra:la]
temple	chrám (m)	[xra:m]
church	kostel (m)	[kostɛl]

college	vysoká škola (ž)	[vɪsoka: ʃkola]
university	univerzita (ž)	[unɪvɛrzɪta]
school	škola (ž)	[ʃkola]

hotel	hotel (m)	[hotɛl]
bank	banka (ž)	[baŋka]
embassy	velvyslanectví (s)	[vɛlvɪslanɛtstvi:]
travel agency	cestovní kancelář (ž)	[tsɛstovni: kantsɛla:rʃ]

subway	metro (s)	[mɛtro]
hospital	nemocnice (ž)	[nɛmotsnɪtsɛ]
gas station	benzínová stanice (ž)	[bɛnzi:nova: stanɪtsɛ]
parking lot	parkoviště (s)	[parkovɪʃte]

ENTRANCE	VCHOD	[vxot]
EXIT	VÝCHOD	[vi:xot]
PUSH	TAM	[tam]
PULL	SEM	[sɛm]
OPEN	OTEVŘENO	[otɛvrʒɛno]
CLOSED	ZAVŘENO	[zavrʒɛno]

monument	památka (ž)	[pama:tka]
fortress	pevnost (ž)	[pɛvnost]
palace	palác (m)	[pala:ts]
medieval (adj)	středověký	[strʃɛdoveki:]

ancient (adj)	starobylý	[starobɪli:]
national (adj)	národní	[na:rodni:]
famous (monument, etc.)	známý	[zna:mi:]

9. Money. Finances

money	peníze (m mn)	[pɛni:zɛ]
coin	mince (ž)	[mɪnʦɛ]
dollar	dolar (m)	[dolar]
euro	euro (s)	[ɛuro]

ATM	bankomat (m)	[baŋkomat]
currency exchange	směnárna (ž)	[smnena:rna]
exchange rate	kurz (m)	[kurs]
cash	hotové peníze (m mn)	[hotovɛ: pɛni:zɛ]

How much?	Kolik?	[kolɪk]
to pay (vi, vt)	platit	[platɪt]
payment	platba (ž)	[platba]
change (give the ~)	peníze (m mn) nazpět	[pɛni:zɛ naspet]

price	cena (ž)	[ʦɛna]
discount	sleva (ž)	[slɛva]
cheap (adj)	levný	[lɛvni:]
expensive (adj)	drahý	[drahi:]

bank	banka (ž)	[baŋka]
account	účet (m)	[u:ʧɛt]
credit card	kreditní karta (ž)	[krɛdɪtni: karta]
check	šek (m)	[ʃɛk]
to write a check	vystavit šek	[vɪstavɪt ʃɛk]
checkbook	šeková knížka (ž)	[ʃɛkova: kni:ʃka]

debt	dluh (m)	[dlux]
debtor	dlužník (m)	[dluʒni:k]
to lend (money)	půjčit	[pu:jʧɪt]
to borrow (vi, vt)	půjčit si	[pu:jʧɪt sɪ]

to rent (~ a tuxedo)	vypůjčit si	[vɪpu:jʧɪt sɪ]
on credit (adv)	na splátky	[na spla:tkɪ]
wallet	náprsní taška (ž)	[na:prsni: taʃka]
safe	trezor (m)	[trɛzor]
inheritance	dědictví (s)	[dedɪtstvi:]
fortune (wealth)	majetek (m)	[majɛtɛk]

tax	daň (ž)	[danʲ]
fine	pokuta (ž)	[pokuta]
to fine (vt)	pokutovat	[pokutovat]
wholesale (adj)	velkoobchodní	[vɛlkoobxodni:]
retail (adj)	maloobchodní	[maloobxodni:]

| to insure (vt) | pojišťovat | [pojɪʃťovat] |
| insurance | pojistka (ž) | [pojɪstka] |

capital	kapitál (m)	[kapɪta:l]
turnover	obrat (m)	[obrat]
stock (share)	akcie (ž)	[aktsɪe]
profit	zisk (m)	[zɪsk]
profitable (adj)	ziskový	[zɪskovi:]

crisis	krize (ž)	[krɪzɛ]
bankruptcy	bankrot (m)	[baŋkrot]
to go bankrupt	zbankrotovat	[zbaŋkrotovat]

accountant	účetní (m, ž)	[u:tʃɛtni:]
salary	mzda (ž)	[mzda]
bonus (money)	prémie (ž)	[prɛ:mɪe]

10. Transportation

bus	autobus (m)	[autobus]
streetcar	tramvaj (ž)	[tramvaj]
trolley bus	trolejbus (m)	[trolɛjbus]

to go by ...	jet	[jɛt]
to get on (~ the bus)	nastoupit do ...	[nastoupɪt do]
to get off ...	vystoupit z ...	[vɪstoupɪt z]

stop (e.g., bus ~)	zastávka (ž)	[zasta:fka]
terminus	konečná stanice (ž)	[konɛtʃna: stanɪtsɛ]
schedule	jízdní řád (m)	[ji:zdni: rʒa:t]
ticket	jízdenka (ž)	[ji:zdɛŋka]
to be late (for ...)	mít zpoždění	[mi:t spoʒdɛni:]

taxi, cab	taxík (m)	[taksi:k]
by taxi	taxíkem	[taksi:kɛm]
taxi stand	stanoviště (s) taxíků	[stanovɪʃte taksi:ku:]

traffic	uliční provoz (m)	[ulɪtʃni: provoz]
rush hour	špička (ž)	[ʃpɪtʃka]
to park (vi)	parkovat se	[parkovat sɛ]

subway	metro (s)	[mɛtro]
station	stanice (ž)	[stanɪtsɛ]
train	vlak (m)	[vlak]
train station	nádraží (s)	[na:draʒi:]
rails	koleje (ž mn)	[kolɛjɛ]
compartment	oddělení (s)	[oddɛlɛni:]
berth	lůžko (s)	[lu:ʃko]
airplane	letadlo (s)	[lɛtadlo]
air ticket	letenka (ž)	[lɛtɛŋka]

| airline | letecká společnost (ž) | [lɛtɛtska: spolɛtʃnost] |
| airport | letiště (s) | [lɛtɪʃte] |

flight (act of flying)	let (m)	[lɛt]
luggage	zavazadla (s mn)	[zavazadla]
luggage cart	vozík (m) na zavazadla	[vozi:k na zavazadla]

ship	loď (ž)	[lotʲ]
cruise ship	linková loď (ž)	[lɪŋkova: lotʲ]
yacht	jachta (ž)	[jaxta]
boat (flat-bottomed ~)	loďka (ž)	[lotʲka]

captain	kapitán (m)	[kapɪta:n]
cabin	kajuta (ž)	[kajuta]
port (harbor)	přístav (m)	[prʃi:staf]

bicycle	kolo (s)	[kolo]
scooter	skútr (m)	[sku:tr]
motorcycle, bike	motocykl (m)	[mototsɪkl]
pedal	pedál (m)	[pɛda:l]
pump	pumpa (ž)	[pumpa]
wheel	kolo (s)	[kolo]

automobile, car	auto (s)	[auto]
ambulance	sanitka (ž)	[sanɪtka]
truck	náklaďák (m)	[na:kladʲa:k]
used (adj)	ojetý	[oeti:]
car crash	havárie (ž)	[hava:rɪe]
repair	oprava (ž)	[oprava]

11. Food. Part 1

meat	maso (s)	[maso]
chicken	slepice (ž)	[slɛpɪtsɛ]
duck	kachna (ž)	[kaxna]

pork	vepřové (s)	[vɛprʃovɛ:]
veal	telecí (s)	[tɛlɛtsi:]
lamb	skopové (s)	[skopovɛ:]
beef	hovězí (s)	[hovezi:]

sausage (bologna, etc.)	salám (m)	[sala:m]
egg	vejce (s)	[vɛjtsɛ]
fish	ryby (ž mn)	[rɪbɪ]
cheese	sýr (m)	[si:r]
sugar	cukr (m)	[tsukr]
salt	sůl (ž)	[su:l]

| rice | rýže (ž) | [ri:ʒe] |
| pasta (macaroni) | makaróny (m mn) | [makaro:nɪ] |

butter	máslo (s)	[ma:slo]
vegetable oil	olej (m)	[olɛj]
bread	chléb (m)	[xlɛ:p]
chocolate (n)	čokoláda (ž)	[ʧokola:da]

wine	víno (s)	[vi:no]
coffee	káva (ž)	[ka:va]
milk	mléko (s)	[mlɛ:ko]
juice	šťáva (ž), džus (m)	[ʃťa:va], [dʒus]
beer	pivo (s)	[pɪvo]
tea	čaj (m)	[ʧaj]

tomato	rajské jablíčko (s)	[rajskɛ: jabli:ʧko]
cucumber	okurka (ž)	[okurka]
carrot	mrkev (ž)	[mrkɛf]
potato	brambory (ž mn)	[bramborɪ]
onion	cibule (ž)	[ʦɪbulɛ]
garlic	česnek (m)	[ʧɛsnɛk]

cabbage	zelí (s)	[zɛli:]
beet	červená řepa (ž)	[ʧɛrvena: rʒɛpa]
eggplant	lilek (m)	[lɪlɛk]
dill	kopr (m)	[koprɪ]
lettuce	salát (m)	[sala:t]
corn (maize)	kukuřice (ž)	[kukurʒɪʦɛ]

fruit	ovoce (s)	[ovoʦɛ]
apple	jablko (s)	[jablko]
pear	hruška (ž)	[hruʃka]
lemon	citrón (m)	[ʦɪtro:n]
orange	pomeranč (m)	[pomɛranʧ]
strawberry (garden ~)	zahradní jahody (ž mn)	[zahradni: jahodɪ]

plum	švestka (ž)	[ʃvɛstka]
raspberry	maliny (ž mn)	[malɪnɪ]
pineapple	ananas (m)	[ananas]
banana	banán (m)	[bana:n]
watermelon	vodní meloun (m)	[vodni: mɛloun]
grape	hroznové víno (s)	[hroznovɛ: vi:no]
melon	cukrový meloun (m)	[ʦukrovi: mɛloun]

12. Food. Part 2

cuisine	kuchyně (ž)	[kuxɪne]
recipe	recept (m)	[rɛʦɛpt]
food	jídlo (s)	[ji:dlo]

to have breakfast	snídat	[sni:dat]
to have lunch	obědvat	[obedvat]
to have dinner	večeřet	[vɛʧɛrʒɛt]

taste, flavor	chuť (ž)	[xuťⁱ]
tasty (adj)	chutný	[xutni:]
cold (adj)	studený	[studɛni:]
hot (adj)	teplý	[tɛpli:]
sweet (sugary)	sladký	[slatki:]
salty (adj)	slaný	[slani:]

sandwich (bread)	obložený chlebíček (m)	[obloʒeni: xlɛbi:ʧɛk]
side dish	příloha (ž)	[prʃi:loha]
filling (for cake, pie)	nádivka (ž)	[na:dɪfka]
sauce	omáčka (ž)	[oma:ʧka]
piece (of cake, pie)	kousek (m)	[kousɛk]

diet	dieta (ž)	[dɪeta]
vitamin	vitamín (m)	[vɪtami:n]
calorie	kalorie (ž)	[kalorɪe]
vegetarian (n)	vegetarián (m)	[vɛgɛtarɪa:n]

restaurant	restaurace (ž)	[rɛstauraʦɛ]
coffee house	kavárna (ž)	[kava:rna]
appetite	chuť (ž) k jídlu	[xuťⁱ k ji:dlu]
Enjoy your meal!	Dobrou chuť!	[dobrou xuťⁱ]

waiter	číšník (m)	[ʧʃi:ʃni:k]
waitress	číšnice (ž)	[ʧʃi:ʃnɪʦɛ]
bartender	barman (m)	[barman]
menu	jídelní lístek (m)	[ji:dɛlni: li:stɛk]

spoon	lžíce (ž)	[lʒi:ʦɛ]
knife	nůž (m)	[nu:ʃ]
fork	vidlička (ž)	[vɪdlɪʧka]
cup (e.g., coffee ~)	šálek (m)	[ʃa:lɛk]

plate (dinner ~)	talíř (m)	[tali:rʃ]
saucer	talířek (m)	[tali:rʒɛk]
napkin (on table)	ubrousek (m)	[ubrousɛk]
toothpick	párátko (s)	[pa:ra:tko]

to order (meal)	objednat si	[objɛdnat sɪ]
course, dish	jídlo (s)	[ji:dlo]
portion	porce (ž)	[porʦɛ]
appetizer	předkrm (m)	[prʃɛtkrm]
salad	salát (m)	[sala:t]
soup	polévka (ž)	[polɛ:fka]

dessert	desert (m)	[dɛsɛrt]
jam (whole fruit jam)	zavařenina (ž)	[zavarʒɛnɪna]
ice-cream	zmrzlina (ž)	[zmrzlɪna]

check	účet (m)	[u:ʧɛt]
to pay the check	zaplatit účet	[zaplatɪt u:ʧɛt]
tip	spropitné (s)	[spropɪtnɛ:]

13. House. Apartment. Part 1

house	**dům** (m)	[duːm]
country house	**venkovský dům** (m)	[vɛŋkovski: duːm]
villa (seaside ~)	**vila** (ž)	[vɪla]
floor, story	**poschodí** (s)	[posxodiː]
entrance	**vchod** (m)	[vxot]
wall	**stěna** (ž)	[stena]
roof	**střecha** (ž)	[strʃɛxa]
chimney	**komín** (m)	[komiːn]
attic (storage place)	**půda** (ž)	[puːda]
window	**okno** (s)	[okno]
window ledge	**parapet** (m)	[parapɛt]
balcony	**balkón** (m)	[balkoːn]
stairs (stairway)	**schodiště** (s)	[sxodɪʃte]
mailbox	**poštovní schránka** (ž)	[poʃtovni: sxra:ŋka]
garbage can	**popelnice** (ž)	[popɛlnɪtsɛ]
elevator	**výtah** (m)	[viːtax]
electricity	**elektřina** (ž)	[ɛlɛktrʃɪna]
light bulb	**žárovka** (ž)	[ʒaːrofka]
switch	**vypínač** (m)	[vɪpiːnatʃ]
wall socket	**zásuvka** (ž)	[zaːsufka]
fuse	**pojistka** (ž)	[pojɪstka]
door	**dveře** (ž mn)	[dvɛrʒɛ]
handle, doorknob	**klika** (ž)	[klɪka]
key	**klíč** (m)	[kliːtʃ]
doormat	**kobereček** (m)	[kobɛrɛtʃɛk]
door lock	**zámek** (m)	[zaːmɛk]
doorbell	**zvonek** (m)	[zvonɛk]
knock (at the door)	**klepání** (s)	[klɛpaːniː]
to knock (vi)	**klepat**	[klɛpat]
peephole	**kukátko** (s)	[kukaːtko]
yard	**dvůr** (m)	[dvuːr]
garden	**zahrada** (ž)	[zahrada]
swimming pool	**bazén** (m)	[bazɛːn]
gym (home gym)	**tělocvična** (ž)	[telotsvɪtʃna]
tennis court	**tenisový kurt** (m)	[tɛnɪsoviː kurt]
garage	**garáž** (ž)	[garaːʃ]
private property	**soukromé vlastnictví** (s)	[soukromɛː vlastnɪtstviː]
warning sign	**výstražný nápis** (m)	[viːstraʒniː naːpɪs]
security	**stráž** (ž)	[straːʃ]
security guard	**strážce** (m)	[straːʒtsɛ]
renovations	**oprava** (ž)	[oprava]

to renovate (vt)	**dělat opravu**	[delat opravu]
to put in order	**dávat do pořádku**	[daːvat do porʒaːtku]
to paint (~ a wall)	**natírat**	[natiːrat]
wallpaper	**tapety** (ž mn)	[tapɛtɪ]
to varnish (vt)	**lakovat**	[lakovat]

pipe	**trubka** (ž)	[trupka]
tools	**nástroje** (m mn)	[naːstrojɛ]
basement	**sklep** (m)	[sklɛp]
sewerage (system)	**kanalizace** (ž)	[kanalɪzatsɛ]

14. House. Apartment. Part 2

apartment	**byt** (m)	[bɪt]
room	**pokoj** (m)	[pokoj]
bedroom	**ložnice** (ž)	[loʒnɪtsɛ]
dining room	**jídelna** (ž)	[jiːdɛlna]

living room	**přijímací pokoj** (m)	[prʃɪjiːmatsi: pokoj]
study (home office)	**pracovna** (ž)	[pratsovna]
entry room	**předsíň** (ž)	[prʃɛtsiːnʲ]
bathroom (room with	**koupelna** (ž)	[koupɛlna]
a bath or shower)		

half bath	**záchod** (m)	[zaːxot]

floor	**podlaha** (ž)	[podlaha]
ceiling	**strop** (m)	[strop]

to dust (vt)	**utírat prach**	[utiːrat prax]
vacuum cleaner	**vysavač** (m)	[vɪsavatʃ]
to vacuum (vt)	**vysávat**	[vɪsaːvat]

mop	**mop** (m)	[mop]
dust cloth	**hadr** (m)	[hadr]
short broom	**koště** (s)	[koʃte]
dustpan	**lopatka** (ž) **na smetí**	[lopatka na smɛtiː]

furniture	**nábytek** (m)	[naːbɪtɛk]
table	**stůl** (m)	[stuːl]
chair	**židle** (ž)	[ʒɪdlɛ]
armchair	**křeslo** (s)	[krʃɛslo]

bookcase	**knihovna** (ž)	[knɪhovna]
shelf	**police** (ž)	[polɪtsɛ]
wardrobe	**skříň** (ž)	[skrʃiːnʲ]

mirror	**zrcadlo** (s)	[zrtsadlo]
carpet	**koberec** (m)	[kobɛrɛts]
fireplace	**krb** (m)	[krp]
drapes	**záclony** (ž mn)	[zaːtslonɪ]

| table lamp | stolní lampa (ž) | [stolni: lampa] |
| chandelier | lustr (m) | [lustr] |

kitchen	kuchyně (ž)	[kuxɪne]
gas stove (range)	plynový sporák (m)	[plɪnovi: spora:k]
electric stove	elektrický sporák (m)	[ɛlɛktrɪtski: spora:k]
microwave oven	mikrovlnná pec (ž)	[mɪkrovlnna: pɛts]

refrigerator	lednička (ž)	[lɛdnɪtʃka]
freezer	mrazicí komora (ž)	[mrazɪtsi: komora]
dishwasher	myčka (ž) nádobí	[mɪtʃka na:dobi:]
faucet	kohout (m)	[kohout]

meat grinder	mlýnek (m) na maso	[mli:nɛk na maso]
juicer	odšťavňovač (m)	[otʃtʲavnʲovatʃ]
toaster	opékač (m) topinek	[opɛ:katʃ topɪnɛk]
mixer	mixér (m)	[mɪksɛ:r]

coffee machine	kávovar (m)	[ka:vovar]
kettle	čajník (m)	[tʃajni:k]
teapot	čajová konvice (ž)	[tʃajova: konvɪtsɛ]

TV set	televizor (m)	[tɛlɛvɪzor]
VCR (video recorder)	videomagnetofon (m)	[vɪdɛomagnɛtofon]
iron (e.g., steam ~)	žehlička (ž)	[ʒehlɪtʃka]
telephone	telefon (m)	[tɛlɛfon]

15. Professions. Social status

director	ředitel (m)	[rʒɛdɪtɛl]
superior	vedoucí (m)	[vɛdoutsi:]
president	prezident (m)	[prɛzɪdɛnt]
assistant	pomocník (m)	[pomotsni:k]
secretary	sekretář (m)	[sɛkrɛta:rʃ]

owner, proprietor	majitel (m)	[majɪtɛl]
partner	partner (m)	[partnɛr]
stockholder	akcionář (m)	[aktsɪona:rʃ]

businessman	byznysmen (m)	[bɪznɪsmen]
millionaire	milionář (m)	[mɪlɪona:rʃ]
billionaire	miliardář (m)	[mɪlɪarda:rʃ]

actor	herec (m)	[hɛrɛts]
architect	architekt (m)	[arxɪtɛkt]
banker	bankéř (m)	[baŋkɛ:rʃ]
broker	broker (m)	[brokɛr]

| veterinarian | zvěrolékař (m) | [zverolɛ:karʃ] |
| doctor | lékař (m) | [lɛ:karʃ] |

chambermaid	pokojská (ž)	[pokojska:]
designer	návrhář (m)	[na:vrha:rʃ]
correspondent	zpravodaj (m)	[spravodaj]
delivery man	kurýr (m)	[kuri:r]

electrician	elektromontér (m)	[ɛlɛktromontɛ:r]
musician	hudebník (m)	[hudɛbni:k]
babysitter	chůva (ž)	[xu:va]
hairdresser	holič (m), kadeřník (m)	[holɪtʃ], [kadɛrʒni:k]
herder, shepherd	pasák (m)	[pasa:k]

singer (masc.)	zpěvák (m)	[speva:k]
translator	překladatel (m)	[prʃɛkladatɛl]
writer	spisovatel (m)	[spɪsovatɛl]
carpenter	tesař (m)	[tɛsarʃ]
cook	kuchař (m)	[kuxarʃ]

fireman	hasič (m)	[hasɪtʃ]
police officer	policista (m)	[polɪtsɪsta]
mailman	listonoš (m)	[lɪstonoʃ]
programmer	programátor (m)	[programa:tor]
salesman (store staff)	prodavač (m)	[prodavatʃ]

worker	dělník (m)	[delni:k]
gardener	zahradník (m)	[zahradni:k]
plumber	instalatér (m)	[ɪnstalatɛ:r]
dentist	stomatolog (m)	[stomatolog]
flight attendant (fem.)	letuška (ž)	[lɛtuʃka]

dancer (masc.)	tanečník (m)	[tanɛtʃni:k]
bodyguard	osobní strážce (m)	[osobni: stra:ʒtsɛ]
scientist	vědec (m)	[vedɛts]
schoolteacher	učitel (m)	[utʃɪtɛl]

farmer	farmář (m)	[farma:rʃ]
surgeon	chirurg (m)	[xɪrurg]
miner	horník (m)	[horni:k]
chef (kitchen chef)	šéfkuchař (m)	[ʃɛ:f kuxarʃ]
driver	řidič (m)	[rʒɪdɪtʃ]

16. Sport

kind of sports	sportovní disciplína (ž)	[sportovni: dɪstsɪpli:na]
soccer	fotbal (m)	[fotbal]
hockey	hokej (m)	[hokɛj]
basketball	basketbal (m)	[baskɛtbal]
baseball	baseball (m)	[bɛjzbol]

| volleyball | volejbal (m) | [volɛjbal] |
| boxing | box (m) | [boks] |

wrestling	zápas (m)	[za:pas]
tennis	tenis (m)	[tɛnɪs]
swimming	plavání (s)	[plava:ni:]

chess	šachy (m mn)	[ʃaxɪ]
running	běh (m)	[bex]
athletics	lehká atletika (ž)	[lɛhka: atlɛtɪka]
figure skating	krasobruslení (s)	[krasobruslɛni:]
cycling	cyklistika (ž)	[ʦɪklɪstɪka]

billiards	kulečník (m)	[kulɛʧni:k]
bodybuilding	kulturistika (ž)	[kulturɪstɪka]
golf	golf (m)	[golf]
scuba diving	potápění (s)	[pota:peni:]
sailing	plachtění (s)	[plaxteni:]
archery	lukostřelba (ž)	[lukostrʃɛlba]

period, half	poločas (m)	[poloʧas]
half-time	poločas (m)	[poloʧas]
tie	remíza (ž)	[rɛmi:za]
to tie (vi)	remizovat	[rɛmɪzovat]

treadmill	běžecký pás (m)	[beʒeʦki: pa:s]
player	hráč (m)	[hra:ʧ]
substitute	náhradník (m)	[na:hradni:k]
substitutes bench	lavice (ž) náhradníků	[lavɪʦɛ na:hradni:ku:]

match	zápas (ž)	[za:pas]
goal	brána (ž)	[bra:na]
goalkeeper	brankář (m)	[braŋka:rʃ]
goal (score)	gól (m)	[go:l]

Olympic Games	Olympijské hry (ž mn)	[olɪmpɪjskɛ: hrɪ]
to set a record	vytvořit rekord	[vɪtvorʒɪt rɛkort]
final	finále (s)	[fɪna:lɛ]
champion	mistr (m)	[mɪstr]
championship	mistrovství (s)	[mɪstrovstvi:]

winner	vítěz (m)	[vi:tez]
victory	vítězství (s)	[vi:tezstvi:]
to win (vi)	vyhrát	[vɪhra:t]
to lose (not win)	prohrát	[prohra:t]
medal	medaile (ž)	[mɛdajlɛ]

first place	první místo (s)	[prvni: mi:sto]
second place	druhé místo (s)	[druhɛ: mi:sto]
third place	třetí místo (s)	[trʃɛti: mi:sto]

stadium	stadión (m)	[stadɪo:n]
fan, supporter	fanoušek (m)	[fanouʃɛk]
trainer, coach	trenér (m)	[trɛnɛ:r]
training	trénink (m)	[trɛ:nɪŋk]

17. Foreign languages. Orthography

language	jazyk (m)	[jazɪk]
to study (vt)	studovat	[studovat]
pronunciation	výslovnost (ž)	[vi:slovnost]
accent	cizí přízvuk (m)	[tsɪzi: prʃi:zvuk]

noun	podstatné jméno (s)	[potsta:tnɛ: jmɛ:no]
adjective	přídavné jméno (s)	[prʃi:davnɛ: jmɛ:no]
verb	sloveso (s)	[slovɛso]
adverb	příslovce (s)	[prʃi:slovtsɛ]

pronoun	zájmeno (s)	[za:jmɛno]
interjection	citoslovce (s)	[tsɪtoslovtsɛ]
preposition	předložka (ž)	[prʃɛdloʃka]

root	slovní základ (m)	[slovni: za:klat]
ending	koncovka (ž)	[kontsofka]
prefix	předpona (ž)	[prʃɛtpona]
syllable	slabika (ž)	[slabɪka]
suffix	přípona (ž)	[prʃi:pona]

stress mark	přízvuk (m)	[prʃi:zvuk]
period, dot	tečka (ž)	[tɛtʃka]
comma	čárka (ž)	[tʃa:rka]
colon	dvojtečka (ž)	[dvojtɛtʃka]
ellipsis	tři tečky (ž mn)	[trʃɪ tɛtʃkɪ]

question	otázka (ž)	[ota:ska]
question mark	otazník (m)	[otazni:k]
exclamation point	vykřičník (m)	[vɪkrʃɪtʃni:k]

in quotation marks	v uvozovkách	[f uvozofka:x]
in parenthesis	v závorkách	[v za:vorkax]
letter	písmeno (s)	[pi:smɛno]
capital letter	velké písmeno (s)	[vɛlkɛ: pi:smɛno]

sentence	věta (ž)	[veta]
group of words	slovní spojení (s)	[slovni: spojɛni:]
expression	výraz (m)	[vi:raz]

subject	podmět (m)	[podmnet]
predicate	přísudek (m)	[prʃi:sudɛk]
line	řádek (m)	[rʒa:dɛk]
paragraph	odstavec (m)	[otstavɛts]

synonym	synonymum (s)	[sɪnonɪmum]
antonym	antonymum (s)	[antonɪmum]
exception	výjimka (ž)	[vi:jɪmka]
to underline (vt)	podtrhnout	[podtrhnout]
rules	pravidla (s mn)	[pravɪdla]

grammar	mluvnice (ž)	[mluvnɪtsɛ]
vocabulary	slovní zásoba (ž)	[slovni: za:soba]
phonetics	hláskosloví (s)	[hla:skoslovi:]
alphabet	abeceda (ž)	[abɛtsɛda]

textbook	učebnice (ž)	[utʃɛbnɪtsɛ]
dictionary	slovník (m)	[slovni:k]
phrasebook	konverzace (ž)	[konvɛrzatsɛ]

word	slovo (s)	[slovo]
meaning	smysl (m)	[smɪsl]
memory	paměť (ž)	[pamnetʲ]

18. The Earth. Geography

the Earth	Země (ž)	[zɛmnɛ]
the globe (the Earth)	zeměkoule (ž)	[zɛmnekoulɛ]
planet	planeta (ž)	[planɛta]

geography	zeměpis (m)	[zɛmnepɪs]
nature	příroda (ž)	[prʃi:roda]
map	mapa (ž)	[mapa]
atlas	atlas (m)	[atlas]

in the north	na severu	[na sɛvɛru]
in the south	na jihu	[na jɪhu]
in the west	na západě	[na za:padɛ]
in the east	na východě	[na vi:xode]

sea	moře (s)	[morʒɛ]
ocean	oceán (m)	[otsɛa:n]
gulf (bay)	záliv (m)	[za:lɪf]
straits	průliv (m)	[pru:lɪf]

continent (mainland)	pevnina (ž)	[pɛvnɪna]
island	ostrov (m)	[ostrof]
peninsula	poloostrov (m)	[poloostrof]
archipelago	souostroví (s)	[souostrovi:]

harbor	přístav (m)	[prʃi:staf]
coral reef	korálový útes (m)	[kora:lovi: u:tɛs]
shore	břeh (m)	[brʒɛx]
coast	pobřeží (s)	[pobrʒɛʒi:]

| flow (flood tide) | příliv (m) | [prʃi:lɪf] |
| ebb (ebb tide) | odliv (m) | [odlɪf] |

latitude	šířka (ž)	[ʃi:rʃka]
longitude	délka (ž)	[dɛ:lka]
parallel	rovnoběžka (ž)	[rovnobeʃka]

equator	rovník (m)	[rovni:k]
sky	obloha (ž)	[obloha]
horizon	horizont (m)	[horɪzont]
atmosphere	atmosféra (ž)	[atmosfɛ:ra]

mountain	hora (ž)	[hora]
summit, top	vrchol (m)	[vrxol]
cliff	skála (ž)	[ska:la]
hill	kopec (m)	[kopɛʦ]

volcano	sopka (ž)	[sopka]
glacier	ledovec (m)	[lɛdovɛʦ]
waterfall	vodopád (m)	[vodopa:t]
plain	rovina (ž)	[rovɪna]

river	řeka (ž)	[rʒɛka]
spring (natural source)	pramen (m)	[pramɛn]
bank (of river)	břeh (m)	[brʒɛx]
downstream (adv)	po proudu	[po proudu]
upstream (adv)	proti proudu	[protɪ proudu]

lake	jezero (s)	[jɛzɛro]
dam	přehrada (ž)	[prʃɛhrada]
canal	průplav (m)	[pru:plaf]
swamp (marshland)	bažina (ž)	[baʒɪna]
ice	led (m)	[lɛt]

19. Countries of the world. Part 1

Europe	Evropa (ž)	[ɛvropa]
European Union	Evropská unie (ž)	[ɛuropska: unɪe]
European (n)	Evropan (m)	[ɛvropan]
European (adj)	evropský	[ɛvropski:]

Austria	Rakousko (s)	[rakousko]
Great Britain	Velká Británie (ž)	[vɛlka: brɪta:nɪe]
England	Anglie (ž)	[anglɪe]
Belgium	Belgie (ž)	[bɛlgɪe]
Germany	Německo (s)	[nemɛʦko]

Netherlands	Nizozemí (s)	[nɪzozɛmi:]
Holland	Holandsko (s)	[holandsko]
Greece	Řecko (s)	[rʒɛʦko]
Denmark	Dánsko (s)	[da:nsko]
Ireland	Irsko (s)	[ɪrsko]

Iceland	Island (m)	[ɪslant]
Spain	Španělsko (s)	[ʃpanelsko]
Italy	Itálie (ž)	[ɪta:lɪe]
Cyprus	Kypr (m)	[kɪpr]

Malta	Malta (ž)	[malta]
Norway	Norsko (s)	[norsko]
Portugal	Portugalsko (s)	[portugalsko]
Finland	Finsko (s)	[fɪnsko]
France	Francie (ž)	[frantsɪe]
Sweden	Švédsko (s)	[ʃvɛːtsko]

Switzerland	Švýcarsko (s)	[ʃviːtsarsko]
Scotland	Skotsko (s)	[skotsko]
Vatican	Vatikán (m)	[vatɪkaːn]
Liechtenstein	Lichtenštejnsko (s)	[lɪxtɛnʃtɛjnsko]
Luxembourg	Lucembursko (s)	[lutsɛmbursko]

Monaco	Monako (s)	[monako]
Albania	Albánie (ž)	[albaːnɪe]
Bulgaria	Bulharsko (s)	[bulharsko]
Hungary	Maďarsko (s)	[madʲarsko]
Latvia	Lotyšsko (s)	[lotɪʃsko]

Lithuania	Litva (ž)	[lɪtva]
Poland	Polsko (s)	[polsko]
Romania	Rumunsko (s)	[rumunsko]
Serbia	Srbsko (s)	[srpsko]
Slovakia	Slovensko (s)	[slovɛnsko]

Croatia	Chorvatsko (s)	[xorvatsko]
Czech Republic	Česko (s)	[tʃɛsko]
Estonia	Estonsko (s)	[ɛstonsko]
Bosnia and Herzegovina	Bosna a Hercegovina (ž)	[bosna a hɛrtsɛgovɪna]
Macedonia (Republic of ~)	Makedonie (ž)	[makɛdonɪe]

Slovenia	Slovinsko (s)	[slovɪnsko]
Montenegro	Černá Hora (ž)	[tʃɛrnaː hora]
Belarus	Bělorusko (s)	[belorusko]
Moldova, Moldavia	Moldavsko (s)	[moldavsko]
Russia	Rusko (s)	[rusko]
Ukraine	Ukrajina (ž)	[ukrajɪna]

20. Countries of the world. Part 2

Asia	Asie (ž)	[azɪe]
Vietnam	Vietnam (m)	[vjɛtnam]
India	Indie (ž)	[ɪndɪe]
Israel	Izrael (m)	[ɪzraɛl]
China	Čína (ž)	[tʃiːna]

Lebanon	Libanon (m)	[lɪbanon]
Mongolia	Mongolsko (s)	[mongolsko]
Malaysia	Malajsie (ž)	[malajzɪe]
Pakistan	Pákistán (m)	[paːkɪstaːn]

Saudi Arabia	Saúdská Arábie (ž)	[sauːdska: araːbɪe]
Thailand	Thajsko (s)	[tajsko]
Taiwan	Tchaj-wan (m)	[tajvan]
Turkey	Turecko (s)	[turɛtsko]
Japan	Japonsko (s)	[japonsko]
Afghanistan	Afghánistán (m)	[afgaːnɪstaːn]
Bangladesh	Bangladéš (m)	[bangladɛːʃ]
Indonesia	Indonésie (ž)	[ɪndonɛːzɪe]
Jordan	Jordánsko (s)	[jordaːnsko]
Iraq	Irák (m)	[ɪraːk]
Iran	Írán (m)	[iːraːn]
Cambodia	Kambodža (ž)	[kambodʒa]
Kuwait	Kuvajt (m)	[kuvajt]
Laos	Laos (m)	[laos]
Myanmar	Barma (ž)	[barma]
Nepal	Nepál (m)	[nɛpaːl]
United Arab Emirates	Spojené arabské emiráty (m mn)	[spojɛnɛː arapskɛː ɛmɪraːtɪ]
Syria	Sýrie (ž)	[siːrɪe]
Palestine	Palestinská autonomie (ž)	[palɛstɪnska: autonomɪe]
South Korea	Jižní Korea (ž)	[jɪʒni: korɛa]
North Korea	Severní Korea (ž)	[severni: korɛa]
United States of America	Spojené státy (m mn) americké	[spojɛnɛː staːtɪ amɛrɪtskɛː]
Canada	Kanada (ž)	[kanada]
Mexico	Mexiko (s)	[mɛksɪko]
Argentina	Argentina (ž)	[argɛntɪna]
Brazil	Brazílie (ž)	[braziːlɪe]
Colombia	Kolumbie (ž)	[kolumbɪe]
Cuba	Kuba (ž)	[kuba]
Chile	Chile (s)	[tʃɪlɛ]
Venezuela	Venezuela (ž)	[vɛnɛzuɛla]
Ecuador	Ekvádor (m)	[ɛkvaːdor]
The Bahamas	Bahamy (ž mn)	[bahamɪ]
Panama	Panama (ž)	[panama]
Egypt	Egypt (m)	[ɛgɪpt]
Morocco	Maroko (s)	[maroko]
Tunisia	Tunisko (s)	[tunɪsko]
Kenya	Keňa (ž)	[kɛnʲa]
Libya	Libye (ž)	[lɪbɪe]
South Africa	Jihoafrická republika (ž)	[jɪhoafrɪtska: rɛpublɪka]
Australia	Austrálie (ž)	[austraːlɪe]
New Zealand	Nový Zéland (m)	[novi: zɛːlant]

21. Weather. Natural disasters

weather	**počasí** (s)	[potʃasi:]
weather forecast	**předpověď** (ž) **počasí**	[prʃɛtpovetʲ potʃasi:]
temperature	**teplota** (ž)	[tɛplota]
thermometer	**teploměr** (m)	[tɛplomner]
barometer	**barometr** (m)	[baromɛtr]
sun	**slunce** (s)	[sluntsɛ]
to shine (vi)	**svítit**	[svi:tɪt]
sunny (day)	**slunečný**	[slunɛtʃni:]
to come up (vi)	**vzejít**	[vzɛji:t]
to set (vi)	**zapadnout**	[zapadnout]
rain	**déšť** (m)	[dɛ:ʃtʲ]
it's raining	**prší**	[prʃi:]
pouring rain	**liják** (m)	[lɪja:k]
rain cloud	**mračno** (s)	[mratʃno]
puddle	**kaluž** (ž)	[kaluʃ]
to get wet (in rain)	**moknout**	[moknout]
thunderstorm	**bouřka** (ž)	[bourʃka]
lightning (~ strike)	**blesk** (m)	[blɛsk]
to flash (vi)	**blýskat se**	[bli:skat sɛ]
thunder	**hřmění** (s)	[hrʒmneni:]
it's thundering	**hřmí**	[hrʒmi:]
hail	**kroupy** (ž mn)	[kroupɪ]
it's hailing	**padají kroupy**	[padaji: kroupɪ]
heat (extreme ~)	**horko** (s)	[horko]
it's hot	**horko**	[horko]
it's warm	**teplo**	[tɛplo]
it's cold	**je zima**	[jɛ zɪma]
fog (mist)	**mlha** (ž)	[mlha]
foggy	**mlhavý**	[mlhavi:]
cloud	**mrak** (m)	[mrak]
cloudy (adj)	**oblačný**	[oblatʃni:]
humidity	**vlhkost** (ž)	[vlxkost]
snow	**sníh** (m)	[sni:x]
it's snowing	**sněží**	[snɛʒi:]
frost (severe ~, freezing cold)	**mráz** (m)	[mra:z]
below zero (adv)	**pod nulou**	[pod nulou]
hoarfrost	**jinovatka** (ž)	[jɪnovatka]
bad weather	**nečas** (m)	[nɛtʃas]
disaster	**katastrofa** (ž)	[katastrofa]
flood, inundation	**povodeň** (ž)	[povodɛnʲ]
avalanche	**lavina** (ž)	[lavɪna]

earthquake	zemětřesení (s)	[zɛmnetrʃɛsɛni:]
tremor, shoke	otřes (m)	[otrʃɛs]
epicenter	epicentrum (s)	[ɛpɪʦɛntrum]
eruption	výbuch (m)	[vi:bux]
lava	láva (ž)	[la:va]

tornado	tornádo (s)	[torna:do]
twister	smršť (ž)	[smrʃtʲ]
hurricane	hurikán (m)	[hurɪka:n]
tsunami	tsunami (s)	[tsunamɪ]
cyclone	cyklón (m)	[ʦiklo:n]

22. Animals. Part 1

animal	zvíře (s)	[zvi:rʒɛ]
predator	šelma (ž)	[ʃɛlma]

tiger	tygr (m)	[tɪgr]
lion	lev (m)	[lɛf]
wolf	vlk (m)	[vlk]
fox	liška (ž)	[lɪʃka]
jaguar	jaguár (m)	[jagua:r]

lynx	rys (m)	[rɪs]
coyote	kojot (m)	[kojot]
jackal	šakal (m)	[ʃakal]
hyena	hyena (ž)	[hɪena]

squirrel	veverka (ž)	[vɛvɛrka]
hedgehog	ježek (m)	[jɛʒek]
rabbit	králík (m)	[kra:li:k]
raccoon	mýval (m)	[mi:val]

hamster	křeček (m)	[krʃɛtʃɛk]
mole	krtek (m)	[krtɛk]
mouse	myš (ž)	[mɪʃ]
rat	krysa (ž)	[krɪsa]
bat	netopýr (m)	[nɛtopi:r]

beaver	bobr (m)	[bobr]
horse	kůň (m)	[ku:nʲ]
deer	jelen (m)	[jɛlɛn]
camel	velbloud (m)	[vɛlblout]
zebra	zebra (ž)	[zɛbra]

whale	velryba (ž)	[vɛlrɪba]
seal	tuleň (m)	[tulɛnʲ]
walrus	mrož (m)	[mroʃ]
dolphin	delfín (m)	[dɛlfi:n]
bear	medvěd (m)	[mɛdvet]

monkey	opice (ž)	[opɪtsɛ]
elephant	slon (m)	[slon]
rhinoceros	nosorožec (m)	[nosoroʒɛts]
giraffe	žirafa (ž)	[ʒɪrafa]

hippopotamus	hroch (m)	[hrox]
kangaroo	klokan (m)	[klokan]
cat	kočka (ž)	[kotʃka]
dog	pes (m)	[pɛs]

cow	kráva (ž)	[kraːva]
bull	býk (m)	[biːk]
sheep (ewe)	ovce (ž)	[ovtsɛ]
goat	koza (ž)	[koza]

donkey	osel (m)	[osɛl]
pig, hog	prase (s)	[prasɛ]
hen (chicken)	slepice (ž)	[slɛpɪtsɛ]
rooster	kohout (m)	[kohout]

duck	kachna (ž)	[kaxna]
goose	husa (ž)	[husa]
turkey (hen)	krůta (ž)	[kruːta]
sheepdog	vlčák (m)	[vltʃaːk]

23. Animals. Part 2

bird	pták (m)	[ptaːk]
pigeon	holub (m)	[holup]
sparrow	vrabec (m)	[vrabɛts]
tit (great tit)	sýkora (ž)	[siːkora]
magpie	straka (ž)	[straka]

eagle	orel (m)	[orɛl]
hawk	jestřáb (m)	[jɛstrʃaːp]
falcon	sokol (m)	[sokol]

swan	labuť (ž)	[labutʲ]
crane	jeřáb (m)	[jɛrʒaːp]
stork	čáp (m)	[tʃaːp]
parrot	papoušek (m)	[papouʃɛk]
peacock	páv (m)	[paːf]
ostrich	pštros (m)	[pʃtros]

heron	volavka (ž)	[volafka]
nightingale	slavík (m)	[slaviːk]
swallow	vlaštovka (ž)	[vlaʃtofka]
woodpecker	datel (m)	[datɛl]
cuckoo	kukačka (ž)	[kukatʃka]
owl	sova (ž)	[sova]

penguin	**tučňák** (m)	[tutʃnʲaːk]
tuna	**tuňák** (m)	[tunʲaːk]
trout	**pstruh** (m)	[pstrux]
eel	**úhoř** (m)	[uːhorʃ]

shark	**žralok** (m)	[ʒralok]
crab	**krab** (m)	[krap]
jellyfish	**medúza** (ž)	[mɛduːza]
octopus	**chobotnice** (ž)	[xobotnɪtsɛ]

starfish	**hvězdice** (ž)	[hvezdɪtsɛ]
sea urchin	**ježovka** (ž)	[jɛʒofka]
seahorse	**mořský koníček** (m)	[morʃski koniːtʃɛk]
shrimp	**kreveta** (ž)	[krɛvɛta]

snake	**had** (m)	[hat]
viper	**zmije** (ž)	[zmɪjɛ]
lizard	**ještěrka** (ž)	[jɛʃterka]
iguana	**leguán** (m)	[lɛguaːn]
chameleon	**chameleón** (m)	[xamɛlɛoːn]
scorpion	**štír** (m)	[ʃtiːr]

turtle	**želva** (ž)	[ʒelva]
frog	**žába** (ž)	[ʒaːba]
crocodile	**krokodýl** (m)	[krokodiːl]

insect, bug	**hmyz** (m)	[hmɪz]
butterfly	**motýl** (m)	[motiːl]
ant	**mravenec** (m)	[mravɛnɛts]
fly	**moucha** (ž)	[mouxa]

mosquito	**komár** (m)	[komaːr]
beetle	**brouk** (m)	[brouk]
bee	**včela** (ž)	[vtʃɛla]
spider	**pavouk** (m)	[pavouk]

24. Trees. Plants

tree	**strom** (m)	[strom]
birch	**bříza** (ž)	[brʒiːza]
oak	**dub** (m)	[dup]
linden tree	**lípa** (ž)	[liːpa]
aspen	**osika** (ž)	[osɪka]

maple	**javor** (m)	[javor]
spruce	**smrk** (m)	[smrk]
pine	**borovice** (ž)	[borovɪtsɛ]
cedar	**cedr** (m)	[tsɛdr]
poplar	**topol** (m)	[topol]
rowan	**jeřáb** (m)	[jɛrʒaːp]

| beech | buk (m) | [buk] |
| elm | jilm (m) | [jɪlm] |

ash (tree)	jasan (m)	[jasan]
chestnut	kaštan (m)	[kaʃtan]
palm tree	palma (ž)	[palma]
bush	keř (m)	[kɛrʃ]

mushroom	houba (ž)	[houba]
poisonous mushroom	jedovatá houba (ž)	[jɛdovata: houba]
cep (Boletus edulis)	hřib (m)	[hrʒɪp]
russula	holubinka (ž)	[holubɪŋka]
fly agaric	muchomůrka (ž) červená	[muxomu:rka tʃɛrvɛna:]
death cap	prašivka (ž)	[praʃɪfka]
flower	květina (ž)	[kvetɪna]
bouquet (of flowers)	kytice (ž)	[kɪtɪtsɛ]
rose (flower)	růže (ž)	[ru:ʒe]
tulip	tulipán (m)	[tulɪpa:n]
carnation	karafiát (m)	[karafɪa:t]

camomile	heřmánek (m)	[hɛrʒma:nɛk]
cactus	kaktus (m)	[kaktus]
lily of the valley	konvalinka (ž)	[konvalɪŋka]
snowdrop	sněženka (ž)	[sneʒeŋka]
water lily	leknín (m)	[lɛkni:n]

conservatory (greenhouse)	oranžérie (ž)	[oranʒe:rɪe]
lawn	trávník (m)	[tra:vni:k]
flowerbed	květinový záhonek (m)	[kvetɪnovi: za:honɛk]
plant	rostlina (ž)	[rostlɪna]
grass	tráva (ž)	[tra:va]
leaf	list (m)	[lɪst]
petal	okvětní lístek (m)	[okvetni: li:stɛk]
stem	stéblo (s)	[stɛ:blo]
young plant (shoot)	výhonek (m)	[vi:honɛk]

cereal crops	obilniny (ž mn)	[obɪlnɪnɪ]
wheat	pšenice (ž)	[pʃenɪtsɛ]
rye	žito (s)	[ʒɪto]
oats	oves (m)	[ovɛs]

millet	jáhly (ž mn)	[ja:hlɪ]
barley	ječmen (m)	[jɛtʃmɛn]
corn	kukuřice (ž)	[kukurʒɪtsɛ]
rice	rýže (ž)	[ri:ʒe]

25. Various useful words

| balance (of situation) | rovnováha (ž) | [rovnova:ha] |
| base (basis) | základna (ž) | [za:kladna] |

beginning	**začátek** (m)	[zatʃaːtɛk]
category	**kategorie** (ž)	[katɛgorɪe]
choice	**volba** (ž)	[volba]
coincidence	**shoda** (ž)	[sxoda]
comparison	**srovnání** (s)	[srovnaːniː]
degree (extent, amount)	**stupeň** (m)	[stupɛnʲ]
development	**rozvoj** (m)	[rozvoj]
difference	**rozdíl** (m)	[rozdiːl]
effect (e.g., of drugs)	**efekt** (m)	[ɛfɛkt]
effort (exertion)	**úsilí** (s)	[uːsɪliː]
element	**prvek** (m)	[prvɛk]
example (illustration)	**příklad** (m)	[prʃiːklat]
fact	**fakt** (m)	[fakt]
help	**pomoc** (ž)	[pomoʦ]
ideal	**ideál** (m)	[ɪdɛaːl]
kind (sort, type)	**druh** (m)	[drux]
mistake, error	**chyba** (ž)	[xɪba]
moment	**moment** (m)	[momɛnt]
obstacle	**překážka** (ž)	[prʃɛkaːʃka]
part (~ of sth)	**část** (ž)	[ʧaːst]
pause (break)	**pauza** (ž)	[pauza]
position	**pozice** (ž)	[pozɪʦɛ]
problem	**problém** (m)	[problɛːm]
process	**proces** (m)	[proʦɛs]
progress	**pokrok** (m)	[pokrok]
property (quality)	**vlastnost** (ž)	[vlastnost]
reaction	**reakce** (ž)	[rɛakʦɛ]
risk	**riziko** (s)	[rɪzɪko]
secret	**tajemství** (s)	[tajɛmstviː]
series	**řada** (ž)	[rʒada]
shape (outer form)	**tvar** (m)	[tvar]
situation	**situace** (ž)	[sɪtuaʦɛ]
solution	**řešení** (s)	[rʒɛʃɛniː]
standard (adj)	**standardní**	[standardniː]
stop (pause)	**přestávka** (ž)	[prʃɛstaːfka]
style	**sloh** (m)	[slox]
system	**systém** (m)	[sɪstɛːm]
table (chart)	**tabulka** (ž)	[tabulka]
tempo, rate	**tempo** (s)	[tɛmpo]
term (word, expression)	**termín** (m)	[tɛrmiːn]
truth (e.g., moment of ~)	**pravda** (ž)	[pravda]

| turn (please wait your ~) | pořadí (s) | [porʒadi:] |
| urgent (adj) | neodkladný | [nɛotkladni:] |

utility (usefulness)	užitek (m)	[uʒɪtɛk]
variant (alternative)	varianta (ž)	[varɪanta]
way (means, method)	způsob (m)	[spu:sop]
zone	pásmo (s)	[pa:smo]

26. Modifiers. Adjectives. Part 1

additional (adj)	dodatečný	[dodatɛtʃni:]
ancient (~ civilization)	starobylý	[starobɪli:]
artificial (adj)	umělý	[umneli:]
bad (adj)	špatný	[ʃpatni:]
beautiful (person)	pěkný	[pekni:]

big (in size)	velký	[vɛlki:]
bitter (taste)	hořký	[horʃki:]
blind (sightless)	slepý	[slɛpi:]
central (adj)	ústřední	[u:strʃɛdni:]

children's (adj)	dětský	[detski:]
clandestine (secret)	podzemní	[podzɛmni:]
clean (free from dirt)	čistý	[tʃɪsti:]
clever (smart)	moudrý	[moudri:]
compatible (adj)	slučitelný	[slutʃɪtɛlni:]

contented (satisfied)	spokojený	[spokojɛni:]
dangerous (adj)	nebezpečný	[nɛbɛzpɛtʃni:]
dead (not alive)	mrtvý	[mrtvi:]
dense (fog, smoke)	hustý	[husti:]
difficult (decision)	těžký	[teʃki:]

dirty (not clean)	špinavý	[ʃpɪnavi:]
easy (not difficult)	snadný	[snadni:]
empty (glass, room)	prázdný	[pra:zdni:]
exact (amount)	přesný	[prʃɛsni:]
excellent (adj)	výborný	[vi:borni:]

excessive (adj)	nadměrný	[nadmnerni:]
exterior (adj)	vnější	[vnejʃi:]
fast (quick)	rychlý	[rɪxli:]
fertile (land, soil)	úrodný	[u:rodni:]
fragile (china, glass)	křehký	[krʃɛxki:]

free (at no cost)	bezplatný	[bɛzplatni:]
fresh (~ water)	sladký	[slatki:]
frozen (food)	zmražený	[zmraʒeni:]
full (completely filled)	plný	[plni:]
happy (adj)	šťastný	[ʃtʲastni:]

hard (not soft)	tvrdý	[tvrdi:]
huge (adj)	obrovský	[obrovski:]
ill (sick, unwell)	nemocný	[nɛmotsni:]
immobile (adj)	nehybný	[nɛhɪbni:]
important (adj)	důležitý	[du:lɛʒɪti:]

interior (adj)	vnitřní	[vnɪtrʃni:]
last (e.g., ~ week)	minulý	[mɪnuli:]
last (final)	poslední	[poslɛdni:]
left (e.g., ~ side)	levý	[lɛvi:]
legal (legitimate)	zákonný	[za:konni:]

light (in weight)	lehký	[lɛhki:]
liquid (fluid)	tekutý	[tɛkuti:]
long (e.g., ~ hair)	dlouhý	[dlouhi:]
loud (voice, etc.)	hlasitý	[hlasɪti:]
low (voice)	tichý	[tɪxi:]

27. Modifiers. Adjectives. Part 2

main (principal)	hlavní	[hlavni:]
matt, matte	matový	[matovi:]
mysterious (adj)	záhadný	[za:hadni:]
narrow (street, etc.)	úzký	[u:ski:]
native (~ country)	rodný	[rodni:]

negative (~ response)	záporný	[za:porni:]
new (adj)	nový	[novi:]
next (e.g., ~ week)	příští	[prʃi:ʃti:]
normal (adj)	normální	[norma:lni:]
not difficult (adj)	snadný	[snadni:]

obligatory (adj)	povinný	[povɪnni:]
old (house)	starý	[stari:]
open (adj)	otevřený	[otɛvrʒɛni:]
opposite (adj)	protilehlý	[protɪlɛhli:]
ordinary (usual)	obvyklý	[obvɪkli:]

original (unusual)	originální	[orɪgɪna:lni:]
personal (adj)	osobní	[osobni:]
polite (adj)	zdvořilý	[zdvorʒɪli:]
poor (not rich)	chudý	[xudi:]

possible (adj)	možný	[moʒni:]
principal (main)	základní	[za:kladni:]
probable (adj)	pravděpodobný	[pravdepodobni:]
prolonged (e.g., ~ applause)	dlouhý	[dlouhi:]
public (open to all)	veřejný	[vɛrʒɛjni:]
rare (adj)	vzácný	[vza:tsni:]

raw (uncooked)	syrový	[sɪrovi:]
right (not left)	pravý	[pravi:]
ripe (fruit)	zralý	[zrali:]

risky (adj)	nebezpečný	[nɛbɛzpɛtʃni:]
sad (~ look)	smutný	[smutni:]
second hand (adj)	použitý	[pouʒiti:]
shallow (water)	mělký	[mnelki:]
sharp (blade, etc.)	ostrý	[ostri:]

short (in length)	krátký	[kra:tki:]
similar (adj)	podobný	[podobni:]
small (in size)	malý	[mali:]
smooth (surface)	hladký	[hlatki:]
soft (~ toys)	měkký	[mneki:]

solid (~ wall)	pevný	[pɛvni:]
sour (flavor, taste)	kyselý	[kɪsɛli:]
spacious (house, etc.)	prostorný	[prostorni:]
special (adj)	speciální	[spɛtsɪa:lni:]

straight (line, road)	přímý	[prʃi:mi:]
strong (person)	silný	[sɪlni:]
stupid (foolish)	hloupý	[hloupi:]
superb, perfect (adj)	vynikající	[vɪnɪkaji:tsi:]

sweet (sugary)	sladký	[slatki:]
tan (adj)	opálený	[opa:lɛni:]
tasty (delicious)	chutný	[xutni:]
unclear (adj)	nejasný	[nɛjasni:]

28. Verbs. Part 1

to accuse (vt)	obviňovat	[obvɪnʲovat]
to agree (say yes)	souhlasit	[souhlasɪt]
to announce (vt)	hlásit	[hla:sɪt]
to answer (vi, vt)	odpovídat	[otpovi:dat]
to apologize (vi)	omlouvat se	[omlouvat sɛ]

to arrive (vi)	přijíždět	[prʃɪji:ʒdet]
to ask (~ oneself)	ptát se	[pta:t sɛ]
to be absent	být nepřítomen	[bi:t nɛprʃi:tomɛn]
to be afraid	bát se	[ba:t sɛ]
to be born	narodit se	[narodɪt sɛ]

to be in a hurry	pospíchat	[pospi:xat]
to beat (to hit)	bít	[bi:t]
to begin (vt)	začínat	[zatʃi:nat]
to believe (in God)	věřit	[vɛrʒɪt]
to belong to ...	patřit	[patrʃɪt]

to break (split into pieces)	**lámat**	[la:mat]
to build (vt)	**stavět**	[stavet]
to buy (purchase)	**kupovat**	[kupovat]
can (v aux)	**moci**	[motsɪ]
can (v aux)	**moci**	[motsɪ]
to cancel (call off)	**zrušit**	[zruʃɪt]

to catch (vt)	**chytat**	[xɪtat]
to change (vt)	**změnit**	[zmnenɪt]
to check (to examine)	**zkoušet**	[skouʃɛt]
to choose (select)	**vybírat**	[vɪbi:rat]
to clean up (tidy)	**uklízet**	[ukli:zɛt]

to close (vt)	**zavírat**	[zavi:rat]
to compare (vt)	**porovnávat**	[porovna:vat]
to complain (vi, vt)	**stěžovat si**	[steʒovat sɪ]
to confirm (vt)	**potvrdit**	[potvrdɪt]
to congratulate (vt)	**blahopřát**	[blahoprʃa:t]

to cook (dinner)	**vařit**	[varʒɪt]
to copy (vt)	**zkopírovat**	[skopi:rovat]
to cost (vt)	**stát**	[sta:t]
to count (add up)	**počítat**	[potʃi:tat]
to count on ...	**spoléhat na ...**	[spolɛ:hat na]

to create (vt)	**vytvořit**	[vɪtvorʒɪt]
to cry (weep)	**plakat**	[plakat]
to dance (vi, vt)	**tančit**	[tantʃɪt]
to deceive (vi, vt)	**podvádět**	[podva:det]
to decide (~ to do sth)	**řešit**	[rʒɛʃɪt]

to delete (vt)	**vymazat**	[vɪmazat]
to demand (request firmly)	**žádat**	[ʒa:dat]
to deny (vt)	**popírat**	[popi:rat]
to depend on ...	**záviset**	[za:vɪsɛt]
to despise (vt)	**pohrdat**	[pohrdat]

to die (vi)	**umřít**	[umrʒi:t]
to dig (vt)	**rýt**	[ri:t]
to disappear (vi)	**zmizet**	[zmɪzɛt]
to discuss (vt)	**projednávat**	[projɛdna:vat]
to disturb (vt)	**rušit**	[ruʃɪt]

29. Verbs. Part 2

to dive (vi)	**potápět se**	[pota:pet sɛ]
to divorce (vi)	**rozvést se**	[rozvɛ:st sɛ]
to do (vt)	**dělat**	[delat]
to doubt (have doubts)	**pochybovat**	[poxɪbovat]
to drink (vi, vt)	**pít**	[pi:t]

to drop (let fall)	pouštět	[pouʃtet]
to dry (clothes, hair)	sušit	[suʃɪt]
to eat (vi, vt)	jíst	[ji:st]
to end (~ a relationship)	přerušovat	[prʃɛruʃovat]
to excuse (forgive)	omlouvat	[omlouvat]

to exist (vi)	existovat	[ɛgzɪstovat]
to expect (foresee)	předvídat	[prʃɛdvi:dat]
to explain (vt)	vysvětlovat	[vɪsvetlovat]
to fall (vi)	padat	[padat]
to fight (street fight, etc.)	prát se	[pra:t sɛ]
to find (vt)	nacházet	[naxa:zɛt]

to finish (vt)	končit	[kontʃɪt]
to fly (vi)	letět	[lɛtet]
to forbid (vt)	zakázat	[zaka:zat]
to forget (vi, vt)	zapomínat	[zapomi:nat]
to forgive (vt)	odpouštět	[otpouʃtet]

to get tired	unavovat se	[unavovat sɛ]
to give (vt)	dávat	[da:vat]
to go (on foot)	jít	[ji:t]
to hate (vt)	nenávidět	[nɛna:vɪdet]
to have (vt)	mít	[mi:t]
to have breakfast	snídat	[sni:dat]
to have dinner	večeřet	[vɛtʃɛrʒɛt]
to have lunch	obědvat	[obedvat]

to hear (vt)	slyšet	[slɪʃɛt]
to help (vt)	pomáhat	[poma:hat]
to hide (vt)	schovávat	[sxova:vat]
to hope (vi, vt)	doufat	[doufat]
to hunt (vi, vt)	lovit	[lovɪt]
to hurry (vi)	spěchat	[spexat]

to insist (vi, vt)	trvat	[trvat]
to insult (vt)	urážet	[ura:ʒet]
to invite (vt)	zvát	[zva:t]
to joke (vi)	žertovat	[ʒertovat]
to keep (vt)	zachovávat	[zaxova:vat]

to kill (vt)	zabíjet	[zabi:jɛt]
to know (sb)	znát	[zna:t]
to know (sth)	vědět	[vedet]
to like (I like …)	líbit se	[li:bɪt sɛ]
to look at …	dívat se	[di:vat sɛ]

to lose (umbrella, etc.)	ztrácet	[stra:tsɛt]
to love (sb)	milovat	[mɪlovat]
to make a mistake	mýlit se	[mi:lɪt sɛ]
to meet (vi, vt)	utkávat se	[utka:vat sɛ]
to miss (school, etc.)	zameškávat	[zameʃka:vat]

30. Verbs. Part 3

to obey (vi, vt)	podřídit se	[podrʒi:dɪt sɛ]
to open (vt)	otvírat	[otvi:rat]
to participate (vi)	zúčastnit se	[zu:tʃastnɪt sɛ]
to pay (vi, vt)	platit	[platɪt]
to permit (vt)	dovolovat	[dovolovat]

to play (children)	hrát	[hra:t]
to pray (vi, vt)	modlit se	[modlɪt sɛ]
to promise (vt)	slibovat	[slɪbovat]
to propose (vt)	nabízet	[nabi:zɛt]
to prove (vt)	dokazovat	[dokazovat]
to read (vi, vt)	číst	[tʃi:st]

to receive (vt)	dostat	[dostat]
to rent (sth from sb)	pronajímat si	[pronaji:mat sɪ]
to repeat (say again)	opakovat	[opakovat]
to reserve, to book	rezervovat	[rɛzɛrvovat]
to run (vi)	běžet	[beʒet]

to save (rescue)	zachraňovat	[zaxranʲovat]
to say (~ thank you)	říci	[rʒi:tsɪ]
to see (vt)	vidět	[vɪdet]
to sell (vt)	prodávat	[proda:vat]
to send (vt)	odesílat	[odɛsi:lat]
to shoot (vi)	střílet	[strʃi:lɛt]

to shout (vi)	křičet	[krʃɪtʃɛt]
to show (vt)	ukazovat	[ukazovat]
to sign (document)	podepisovat	[podɛpɪsovat]
to sing (vi)	zpívat	[spi:vat]
to sit down (vi)	sednout si	[sɛdnout sɪ]

to smile (vi)	usmívat se	[usmi:vat sɛ]
to speak (vi, vt)	mluvit	[mluvɪt]
to steal (money, etc.)	krást	[kra:st]
to stop (please ~ calling me)	zastavovat	[zastavovat]
to study (vt)	studovat	[studovat]

to swim (vi)	plavat	[plavat]
to take (vt)	brát	[bra:t]
to talk to ...	mluvit s ...	[mluvɪt s]
to tell (story, joke)	povídat	[povi:dat]
to thank (vt)	děkovat	[dekovat]
to think (vi, vt)	myslit	[mɪslɪt]

to translate (vt)	překládat	[prʃɛkla:dat]
to trust (vt)	důvěřovat	[du:verʒovat]
to try (attempt)	pokoušet se	[pokouʃɛt sɛ]

| to turn (e.g., ~ left) | zatáčet | [zataːtʃɛt] |
| to turn off | vypínat | [vɪpiːnat] |

to turn on	zapínat	[zapiːnat]
to understand (vt)	rozumět	[rozumnet]
to wait (vt)	čekat	[tʃɛkat]
to want (wish, desire)	chtít	[xtiːt]
to work (vi)	pracovat	[pratsovat]
to write (vt)	psát	[psaːt]

Made in United States
Orlando, FL
21 December 2022

27399623R00063